The Life
God Wants
You to Have

Discovering
The Divine Plan When
Human Plans Fail

Dr. Gregory K. Popcak, Ed.D.

A Crossroad Book
The Crossroad Publishing Company
New York

The Crossroad Publishing Company
www.CrossroadPublishing.com

In continuation of our 200-year tradition of independent publishing, The Crossroad Publishing Company proudly offers a variety of books with strong, original voices and diverse perspectives. The viewpoints expressed in our books are not necessarily those of The Crossroad Publishing Company, any of its imprints or of its employees. No claims are made or responsibility assumed for any health or other benefit.

While the stories in this book are based on real events, they are composites. All the names and identifying details have been changed to protect the identities of the people involved.

Printed in the United States of America.
The text of this book is set in Web Fusion
The display face is Apollo & Calisto

Project Management by
The Crossroad Publishing Company
John Jones

For this edition numerous people have shared their talents and ideas, and we gratefully acknowledge Gregory Popcak, who has been most gracious during the course of our cooperation. We thank especially:

Cover design: George Foster   Text scanning and design: Web Fusion
Proofreading: Sylke Jackson   Printing: Versa Press

Message development, text development, package, and market positioning by
The Crossroad Publishing Company

Library of Congress Cataloging-in-Publication Data available from the publisher

ISBN 13: 978-0-8245-2696-2

Books published by The Crossroad Publishing Company may be purchased at special quantity discount rates for classes and institutional use. For information, please e-mail info@CrossroadPublishing.com

Contents

Part One: Getting Started

1. "When I Grow Up . . ."   3

2. You Have to Start with Yourself   23

   – Meaningfulness Quiz   30
   – Intimacy Quiz   40
   – Virtue Quiz   50

Part Two: Walking in F.A.I.T.H.

3. Follow the Rules for Healthy Discernment.   61

4. Act, Even When You Doubt.   78

5. Investigate the Causes of Your Anxiety.   96

6. Take Others into Account.   122

7. Hold On Through Adversity.   143

Part Three: Further Steps

8. Conclusion – Moving from Suffering
   to Surrender   167

9. Epilogue: Finding Strength in Community   194

PART ONE
GETTING STARTED

ONE

When I Grow Up . . .

"I never expected things to turn out like this." Paulette is a forty-four-year-old woman with three children. Her husband, Charles, recently left her for a twenty-five-year-old intern who was working in his law practice. She was devastated.

"I don't even know where to start," she said. "I don't know who to be more angry at. Him, for fooling around on me? Me, for being so stupid not to see it coming? Or God, for letting this all happen?"

* * *

Martin, thirty-seven, is a production control supervisor for the local nail manufacturing plant. He makes a fair-enough living, but he experiences his life as empty and unsatisfying.

"Every morning," he reports, "I wake up and wonder if this is what God really put me here to do. I have to fight to be on time for work, and I can't wait to leave at the end of the day. I know I'm no different from a lot of people, and I should probably just be grateful for what I have, but I can't stop wondering if this is really all there is. When I look back, I never really had a plan for my life.

"I just sorta went where life took me, y' know? Except now, I feel like my work is sucking me dry and I don't have anything left to give my wife and kids. I'm tired and depressed a lot of the time. I'd love to make a change, but I'm not sure what to do or where I'd go."

* * *

Michael has the opposite problem. Ever since he was a young boy, he's known he would be a doctor like his dad.

"It was as if it was preordained," he says. "I would go to med school and enter my dad's internal medicine practice. I killed myself to get the grades I needed and graduated near the top of my class.

"Now I make an enviable living. I have just about anything I want, including professional respect. But after all this time, I am struck by the fact that I despise what I do.

"I wanted to be a doctor because that was what my family wanted for me. I suppose they could have done worse, but I realize now I never had a passion for it. I could make myself do it, but I never really wanted to do it.

"Now, ten years out of medical school, I wish I'd never done it. There are so many other things I would have liked to do better. But I feel like I'm trapped by my success and the expectations everyone puts on me."

* * *

All Rebecca ever wanted was to get married and have a large family. A deeply religious woman, she felt that motherhood was the most important work she could do and wanted it more than anything.

Unfortunately, for years, marriage evaded her. When she was in her early twenties, she had been engaged to a man whom she had dated for five years, but he broke the engagement two months before their wedding. She tried to get on with her life, but she never seemed to find someone with whom she really clicked.

She finally met Joseph when she was thirty-five, and they married within a year. She felt that God was finally granting her heart's deepest wish, but when they tried to have the family she had always wanted, nothing happened.

"The doctors have some big medical name for it," she says, "but it basically means that I won't be able to get pregnant, or sustain a pregnancy if I do. I just don't know what to think. Why would God make me want something so badly for so long only to crush my dream in the end?

"I feel so betrayed. Whenever I've experienced disappointments in the past, I would take them to God. Right now, I'm afraid of him. He did this to me. How can I trust a God who would allow me to suffer like this?"

* * *

Not long ago, a national television commercial for an employment agency showed, in warm, sepia tones, images of children looking like little Rockwellian caricatures as sentimental music played in the background. Against this "isn't life grand?" backdrop, the children stepped into focus one by one to speak. The first proudly announced, "When I grow up. I want to be a 'yes' man."

"When I grow up," said the next, "I want to be downsized." "When I grow up, I want to be stuck in middle-management."

And so on. Poignantly, cheekily, and cynically pointing out something of which many of us are all too well aware: Life does not often turn out to be what we expect it will be.

If we were to continue the theme, we could just as easily add many similar statements.

"When I grow up, I want to be a single parent."

"When I grow up, I want to be alone."

"When I grow up, I want to struggle with illness and disease."

And a million other sad permutations of this theme, many lived out every day by millions of people all around the globe. Maybe even by you.

The truth is, when we are children we do not dream of downsizing, divorce, or disease. We dream of success, of marrying that prince or princess, building a castle together, and filling it with children. We dream of fame, or wealth, or perhaps simply happiness.

But sometimes our dreams don't come true. The prince turns out to be an unrepentant frog after all, the castle is more like a ruin, and no matter how many rainbows we chase, wealth and happiness continue to hide at the end of the *next* rainbow. Yet somehow, through it all, as Christians we are encouraged to hold on to our hope, our faith, and the love of God that—as people are telling us, anyway—continues to call out to us the promise of something better.

Hard-Won Hope

Though we have begun this journey on something of a bittersweet note—the promise of youth frustrated by the pressure of years—I want to state right now that this is a book about hope: not the false hope fostered by wishful thinking, but the hard-won hope of people who have struggled, survived, and lived to know the blessings and peace that God has in store for them for their perseverance. All the people I described at the beginning of this chapter are people I have had the privilege of working with and walking alongside on their road to healing and peace. Every day in my work counseling Christians all over the world, I hear similar stories of people who struggle in faith, who are asking hard questions: Why did God do this to me? What am I supposed to do now? Where is my life going?

The good news is that there are answers to these questions— not general, cookie-cutter answers, but individualized, personal, meaningful, and discernible answers. I too have struggled with similar questions in my life, as I am sure most human beings have. I am grateful that God has allowed me to use the techniques and attitudes I will present in this book to find fortitude in my times of struggle and to help others keep up the fight as well. More importantly, I am grateful that God has shown me how to use these techniques and attitudes to find, and help others discover, the resurrection that comes after facing life's crosses head-on.

In your own life, you may not have experienced circumstances as painful as the ones with which I began this chapter. Of course, some of you may have endured much worse. Regardless of the crosses you have had to carry, or the expectations that remain unfulfilled, I want to assure you that there is hope for your future, there is purpose to your life, and there is a resurrection after this cross.

Romans 8:28 tells us, "We know that in everything God works for good with those who love him, who are called according to his purpose." It is my intention, in this book, to help you confront the disappointments of your life head-on, to face the challenges with courage, and to learn to respond in such a way that God will be able to lead you step-by-step out of your darkness and into the light of his peace and truth.

I have to be honest with you. Life is challenging no matter how much you know, how much faith you have, and how much talent you may possess. There have been many times in my life so far that I have almost been completely crushed. While I do not wish to compare my trials to yours—each person's suffering is certainly unique—I think it is important, in the interest of disclosure, to let you know that I do not write this book from the lofty position of one who has lived the first half of his life entirely unscathed.

Just as I have been blessed abundantly throughout my years, I have also been forced to confront many difficulties. For instance, I have had to deal with the possibility that I might never be able to have children. I have suffered the death of a child. I have lived through several serious illnesses of my wife. And I have endured more than my share of serious professional disasters.

Unfortunately, I am sure that there will be many more times like these to come. But one thing that gives me courage is the knowledge that following each one of these times, God has granted me the ability to see why it was necessary for me to go through that particular dark valley. I seem to be in the enviable position of being able to look back on my life and see how everything adds up, and why it was necessary for me to make even the mistakes I did, so that, ultimately, I could become the person God needed me to be today.

I trust, then, that God will grant me this same gift in the future, the gift of discerning the meaning of my suffering and discovering the point behind my disappointments. That makes all the difference in the world.

I didn't fully appreciate the gift I had been given—I assumed that everybody else was able to look at their life in the same manner—until, through my work as a counselor, I realized how different the perspective I had been given really was. It seems that most people, even deeply, devout Christian people, have a fatalistic view of disappointments and suffering. Too many of us say to ourselves, "Oh, well. That's the way life is. Nothing we can do about it." Or at best, we reason, "Perhaps God has allowed me to go through this so that someday I could be a witness to somebody else."

Well, perhaps that is true. But one thing I have discovered, and have helped others discover, is that in addition to whatever deeper spiritual or social significance our own suffering and disappointments may hold, there is always, always, always, a deep, personal, and discernible message conveyed by the good, bad, and indifferent circumstances through which God leads his children.

Time after time, Scripture refers to Jesus as "Rabbi" and "Teacher." God is the ultimate teacher of life and love. Good teachers, as undoubtedly our Lord must be, do not merely make their students endure lessons; they stand by their students and help them discern the meaning behind those lessons, all so that the students may fulfill the potential they have been given.

Joy—A State of Being

In the course of this book, it will be my hope to help you confront your unfulfilled expectations, discern whether it is more appropriate to pursue or alter those expectations, and discover what it takes to pursue both meaning and intimacy, the pillars upon which joy rests. And that's really what we all want, isn't it? Joy.

Unfortunately, most people confuse joy with happiness, but they are different. Happiness is transient; it is situation-specific. Something pleasurable happens; I am happy. Something unpleasant occurs; I am unhappy.

But joy is a gift of the Holy Spirit, and as such, it is not so much a feeling as a state of being. Joy is the sense of well-being that results from knowing that my life is meaningful and my relationships are intimate. Thus unfulfilled expectations seek to threaten and undermine joy. They cause me to doubt the purpose of my life, to despair about my future, and to be dissatisfied with my relationships.

If you wish to commit yourself to resolving the pain that accompanies unfulfilled expectations, then the first quality you must commit to practicing in your life is joy. You must engage in the dogged pursuit of meaning and intimacy in every aspect of your life and relationships.

Of course, the first step to pursuing joy is pursuing Christ. Without a deep, personal love for Christ and his Church, we cannot hope to discover the meaning of life or the source of intimacy. God is the Author of life and love. We cannot master either unless we are on intimate terms with the Author.

Unfortunately, many of the people with whom I speak have been Christian for years but still do not have a relationship with Christ. I do not mean this as a criticism, only as an observation. They have a longing for God, and a devotion to him, but they do not feel a passion for Christ and his passion returned for them. They cannot sense the prompting of his Spirit, they cannot hear his voice whisper either directly to their hearts or indirectly through the events of their lives, and they cannot see the finger of God pointing out the direction they should go. Because of this lack, they either become confused at the journey's outset, hesitating because they don't know whether they are following God's plan or their own, or they lack the courage to continue down the path once hardship strikes, since their plans tend to be buoyed, not so much by grace as by their own enthusiasm, which is all too susceptible to self-doubt and discouragement from others.

Nevertheless, through it all, I believe, God is calling out to us, asking us, as Pope John Paul II said, to "become who we are." And who are we? Too many of us think we are the incomplete person we see when we look in the mirror. But that is not who we really are. After all, would God really ask us to become *that?*

Of course not. Becoming who we are means spending our lives becoming the people that God had in his mind when he created us. Scripture compares God to a potter. When you are conceived, you are a lump of clay. From that moment forward, you will spend your whole life being molded by the hands of God into what you really are. In fact, though you are a lump of clay right now, you will not become who you really are until the potter finishes forming you at the end of your life and takes you off the wheel so that you can serve him in his house.

We look at ourselves and see the lump of clay. God, on the other hand, acknowledges that he is working with clay, but sees in his mind's eye the work of art we really are. But here is the fun as well as the challenging part: We are not merely passive recipients of God's beneficent hand. God, the potter, actually allows the pots to have a hand in shaping themselves.

In fact, God, who is all-powerful, has remarkably created the world in such a way that he uses us to finish the creative work. If I take the time to learn the intimate mind of the Potter so that I can help to form myself according to the image he has in his mind, then this co-creation can be a truly wonderful and rewarding process. On the other hand, if I don't take the time to really get to know the mind of the potter and I do only what I think the potter wants me to do, then I will inevitably get in his way—which is why we must start our journey with an intimate relationship with God.

Since we are cooperators in God's plan of creation, we need to know the general outline of his plan. Let's take a look at some of the basic points we need to keep in mind for dealing with frustration and disappointment.

1. God loves you.

God loves you. Scripture tells us that even the hairs on your head are numbered (a fairly easy task in my case, sad to say). If God cares about the number of hairs on your head, how dare you think that he doesn't care about something as significant as the purpose for which you were created!

God loves you. You have heard it all before, I know. But when you look around in the middle of the dark forest of disappointment, it is so easy to doubt it. Too often, we think that if God really loves us, we will never suffer. This is simply not the case.

To love someone is to work for that person's good. Sometimes working for another's good means allowing them to struggle so that they can grow in competence, strength, maturity, and virtue.

Imagine a father watching his son play in a "big game" or perform an important part in a play. Sometimes it is harder to tell who is more anxious, the child or the parent. The father may see the nervous child struggling; he may even want to rush to his son and take on that struggle for himself, but doesn't.

Why not? Is it because the father doesn't love his son enough? Is it because he doesn't care about the child's suffering? Of course not. The parent feels the child's pain almost as much as—if not more than—the child. But the father, if he is a good parent, allows the child to struggle so that he will discover the gifts God has given him. Allowing the child to struggle is the most loving thing the parent can do in this circumstance.

And so it is with God. When you are struggling with your own sense of limitation, frustration, and disappointment, God is standing there, quietly cheering you on. "I have given you what you need to rise above this. Use your gifts. I know you can."

We will further discuss this matter later in the book, but for now I need you to remember this: If you are struggling, God has given you the tools to respond in a true and godly way to that struggle. But you will find that way only if you hold on to the fact that he loves you.

If you don't, the darkness that accompanies the feeling of being all alone in the universe will eat you alive. This darkness does not come from God. Fight it. Trust in his love, and press on.

2. God created you for a purpose.

Each one of us was created to fulfill a particular purpose in building up the body of Christ, God's kingdom on earth. We all know this, or say we do, but not everybody grasps the significance of that statement.

Imagine that you purchase an appliance of some sort. As long as you use that appliance in the manner for which it was created it will function well. In a sense, that thing will be content to be used according to its design.

But imagine using it instead in an inappropriate way—for example, using a food processor to pound nails. If you were to use the appliance in this foolish manner, it would not function well. It would fail or at best underperform at the task you were giving it to do, and eventually, it would break down entirely.

In the same way, when we do the tasks for which we were created, and in the manner we were created to do them, we function well, and contentment results. If, on the other hand, we are consumed by work and activities that are not what we were created to do, we will not function well, and to varying degrees, we will be miserable.

Now, it can be difficult to discern exactly what we were created to do. For example, what makes us happy (that is, makes us comfortable in the moment) is not necessarily what will make our lives meaningful, intimate, and therefore joyful. Sometimes, due to the false lessons we have picked up along the way, the lies we have swallowed, and the injuries we have sustained to our psyches, what we think will make us content is completely different from what will actually make us content. Which leads us to the next point.

3. We must want what God wants for our lives more than anything else.

We want so many things. Unfortunately, most of the things we want are simply replacements for the things God created us to truly need in order to function well. God created us to pursue intimacy and meaning, but we are told, often from birth, that it is wrong to expect either from life. Because of this, we seek other things to fill our longings: toys, escapist activity, money, license to do what makes us feel good in the moment without regard for the effect on either those who share our lives or on our own long-term well-being.

What ends up happening, however, is that we become obsessed with those things. The ontological holes (that is, the holes in our very being) that are reserved for God, meaning, and intimacy, we try to fill with things, activity, and comfort. When that doesn't fill the void, we think what is missing is—you guessed it—more things, activity, and comfort (either the active comfort of materialism or the passive comfort of not wanting to be bothered too much by anything outside our comfort zone).

The result is a terrible, obsessive cycle that saps our energy and destroys our lives. Moreover, God will not honor these pursuits of ours (that is, he won't allow them to satisfy us) because they stand between him and us. What ends up happening, then, is that the more we pursue things, activity, and comfort, the more unsatisfied we feel and so the more things, activity, and comfort we pursue to fill that unsatisfied feeling. As Augustine said, "Our hearts are restless, O Lord, until they find their rest in you."

If we want to find fulfillment, then, we must give all our energy to three things.

God

We need to pray about every choice we make and everything we do before, during, and after we do it. Do you pray that your life would be a reflection of what God created you to do and who he created you to be?

Imagine if you could pray that prayer like you meant it every day for the rest of your life. What couldn't you accomplish? By choosing to want what God wants for you, you set yourself on the path to fulfilling the purpose for which you were created, and thus you set yourself on the path to fulfillment.

Another aspect of pursuing God in your life is living a life of virtue. When we practice the virtues in all our actions, God manifests himself and his grace more fully in our lives and relationships—and fulfillment follows. In several of my other books, I give an extensive exercise describing how, specifically, to make decisions using such virtues as the gifts and fruits of the Holy Spirit, the theological virtues of faith, hope, and love, and the cardinal virtues of justice, temperance, prudence, and fortitude. For our purposes, it is enough to say that joy and fulfillment come, in large part, from pursuing God through the virtues that manifest his presence in our lives.

Intimacy

John Paul II wrote, "Love is the fundamental and innate call of every human being." Unfortunately, too many of us are afraid to be truly intimate. Instead, we want to be only as close to others as we are comfortable being. "And don't ask me for any more," we say both to others and to God.

Every time we choose to pursue our own comfort over intimacy, however, we violate one of the purposes for which we were created and we begin to break down. We step onto the obsessive cycle I described above, and we lose ourselves. We become angry, bitter, and ultimately, alone. (This is possible even if we are surrounded by a house full of people.)

If you want to find contentment and joy, then you must choose to want intimacy more than anything, even when it scares you. You must want to share yourself with others as completely as is appropriate and insist that they give you as much as they are capable in return. Then you must work to expand your capacity for giving and receiving love so that you can have even more intimacy in your life. When you do this—and we will discuss more about how in a later chapter—you place yourself on the path to contentment.

Meaning

Meaning in life comes from using the gifts and charisms (that is, spiritual gifts) we have been given as fully as possible, and using them to work for the good of others and the glory of God. So many of us do work or fulfill roles that have nothing to do with the gifts God has given us.

Am I suggesting that you quit your job today? No. But I am suggesting that if you ever hope to find contentment in your life, you will have to identify the gifts you have been given and use them as fully as possible in the place God has put you.

God gave you certain talents and gifts. Every day, pray, "God, thank you for these gifts. I want to use them fully to glorify you and build up your kingdom. Show me how." If you do this continually, God will show you step-by-step how to discover and use the unique gifts he has given you, whatever they are. When you work to use the gifts and talents you have been given—no matter how silly, unrealistic, or irrelevant you think those gifts are—you are beginning to function in the manner for which you were created, and you will be content.

Pursuing God, intimacy, and meaning in your life sets you on the path for true success, for these are the things for which every human being was created. Sometimes pursuing these goods means doing something with your life different from what you currently are doing with it. Often, however, it simply means doing what you are already doing, and with whom you are already doing it, with a new focus.

In the course of this book, we will explore how to know whether God is calling you to move on or calling you to bloom where you are planted. For now, know that when you discover how to use the unique gifts you have been given to facilitate your pursuit of God and intimacy, you are empowered to experience meaning in your life—meaning from which flows the joy that banishes unfulfilled expectations.

4. God cares about your fulfillment.

If it is true that God created you for a purpose, then it is also true that God cares deeply that you fulfill that purpose, for you play an important role in building his kingdom. Likewise, knowing that fulfilling the purpose for which you were created makes you happy, you could also say that God cares deeply about your fulfillment. But there is a catch to this last statement. A qualifier.

When I make this statement, people think I mean that God wants us to be happy, which is only partially true. God is certainly not opposed to our happiness, but what God wants more than anything is for us to be *whole*. Sometimes, in the process of becoming whole (that is, becoming who we truly are), we need to do things and undergo difficult times that will not make us happy in the least.

Through it all, we must remember that while we are God's children, and he loves us very much, and the happiness of his children is important to him, we are also his sick children. Sick children need to receive medicine to be made whole, and sometimes, for us, that medicine comes in the form of trials, setbacks, disappointment, and suffering. If we pursue happiness as an end in itself, that is, in an attempt to avoid the suffering that is necessary for us to undergo in order to become whole, God will not honor our quest for happiness. We will fail miserably and will be miserable for our efforts.

To say that God cares deeply about our fulfillment is to say that God wants us to be happy *as long as we are pursuing virtue, intimacy, and meaning.* If you pursue these three things in your life, then God is rooting for you. As long as you approach the setbacks and challenges you encounter in pursuit of these three things with courage and grace, your fulfillment is assured because you are actualizing the purpose for which you were created—and when a thing functions according to the manner in which it was created, it is content. God cares about your wholeness, and when you are whole—or are at least pursuing wholeness—you will be joyful because your life will have God, intimacy, and meaning. So it is in this sense that God cares about your fulfillment. He cares about the fulfillment that comes from your avoiding mere happy escapism and instead doggedly working to become who you are.

If you ever want to know if God will bless a particular choice or pursuit, ask yourself this simple question: Does the thing you want to give your energy to lead to greater devotion to God and virtue, more intimacy between you and others, or a greater sense of meaning and purpose in your life? The degree to which you can answer yes to all three points is the degree to which you should pursue that activity, knowing that God will bless it. He will bless it because it leads to your wholeness, which in turn leads to your happiness.

5. God believes in you.

Finally, you may be going through a period of your life that is causing you to doubt yourself. We have all been there, and we will probably be there many times in the future. It all comes from not knowing whether or not our talents, gifts, and other resources are really up to the challenge at hand. When we doubt what God has given us—intellect, will, intelligence, discernment, talent, and grace—we fall into confusion and hopelessness. We fall into despair.

If you are going through such a time, I want you to know that God believes in you. God has given you not only all the things we just noted, but also every single breath you take. I don't care whether you feel it is true; as a counselor, I am telling you that feelings can be horribly misleading.

Regardless of what you feel, regardless of what you think is true, the reality is that God believes in you. If he did not, he would not have created you, he would not have gifted you, and he would not sustain you. You are a precious treasure to God, and he believes in you.

Grace is the evidence that God believes in you. Any time you exercise any of the virtues, or the gifts and fruits of the Holy Spirit, you do so because God believes in you enough to give you that gift of hope, or wisdom, or fortitude, or counsel, or knowledge. Every time you receive the Sacrament of Reconciliation, God gives you the grace that says, "I believe in you to leave this place and do better than you did before." Every time you receive Christ's precious Body and Blood in the Eucharist, God expresses his belief in you that you are, indeed, worthy to receive him—not on your own power, but because he has pronounced you "worthy."

God believes in you. *You* don't have to believe in yourself. Just believe in God, and trust that if he has put you in a spot, he will give you the grace to get out of that spot.

As Scripture says, if God is for you, who can be against you? (See Rom 8:31.) Though you are tired, frustrated, unfulfilled, and doubtful, trust in him and he will give you what you need. God believes in you.

Don't you dare doubt it for one second. With every breath you take—and I mean this as literally as possible—I want you to say to yourself, "I believe in God. God believes in me. I believe in God. God believes in me."

It sounds corny, I know, but it won't kill you to try it. In fact, it just might save you. Don't be too prideful to try. The battle for the soul is waged in the mind. Fill your mind with trust in the Lord, and he will fill your soul with the grace you need to rise out of the disappointments you face every day. God believes in you.

Inevitably, however, when I tell people that God believes in them, they respond by saying, "Yes, but what does he believe in me to do?"

The rest of the book will set about answering exactly that question. First, we will explore the secret of living fully in the moment regardless of your circumstances. Then we will assess whether the lack of fulfillment you are experiencing requires a minor adjustment to your life or a major overhaul.

After this assessment, the following chapters will explore the five steps you need to take in order to discover and fulfill all that God has planned for you. Represented by the word FAITH, those five steps are . . .

Follow the Rules for Healthy Discernment.
Act, Even When You Doubt.
Investigate the Causes of Your Anxiety.
Take Others into Account.
Hold On Through Adversity.

Later, we will examine each one of these steps in depth. It is my hope that through the course of this book, God will lead you, step-by-step, out of the darkness in which you find yourself and into the presence of his marvelous light.

Finally, you will discover how to respond to setbacks and catastrophic events that are completely beyond your control.

God wants you to respond even to that kind of event in a manner that allows you to become the person he is calling you to be and to experience the joy that accompanies such a call.

TWO

You Have to Start with Yourself

Jennifer, forty, is a stay-at-home mother of four. Though a college graduate, she jokes that she spent four years pursuing her "MRS." degree since she got married the day after college graduation. She and her husband, Brian, had their first child within the year, and they both decided that they wanted her to be home with the baby.

Generally speaking, Jennifer has been very satisfied with her work as a homemaker and mother of four. Yet there is a part of her, she says, that feels as if she is a stay-at-home mother by default. She often wonders whether she may be missing something by not using her degree in Library and Information Science.

"I love taking care of my husband and my kids," she insists. "But maybe I should be doing more with my gifts than just being the family chauffeur, housekeeper, chief cook, and bottle-washer."

When it comes right down to it, Jennifer feels unfulfilled. Is it time, she asks herself, for a radical change of some sort?

"I don't know what I'd do exactly, but maybe I should try to shake things up in my life. I'm tired of running on autopilot. I'd like to feel a little more alive."

* * *

Roger, forty-four, is experiencing the symptoms of a type of depression called *dysthymia,* the "walking pneumonia" of depressions. It allows him to function while making him irritable about every little thing and sapping the joy from doing even the things he once experienced as highly enjoyable.

"I just wake every morning feeling like it's the 'same stuff, different day.' I am just not happy," he confesses. "I don't know if it's my marriage, my work, or what. I just know I'm not happy, no-how. I have this fantasy that one day I'm gonna do like that Springsteen song and go out for a ride and never come back. I don't mean kill myself or anything, just start all over someplace else. Maybe if I could do it over, I could get it right this time."

Roger pauses for a moment before he issues this challenge to me.

"The thing I need most from our sessions is to figure out when do I know if it's just time to say when? Is there something I'm not doing to make all this work? Or is it time just to say, 'I tried, and I need to move on'?"

* * *

When we feel frustrated in our lives, we experience a natural tendency to want to do something, anything, no matter how rash, to ease the pain. In my years of counseling, I have seen many people make radical shifts in their lives, relationships, and priorities because they came to the conclusion that they were unfulfilled because they had chosen the wrong profession, married the wrong person, or held erroneous beliefs. In some circumstances, these radical shifts were warranted, and in such cases the moves these individuals made were well thought-out and discerned in consultation with responsible others.

Unfortunately, in most cases the opposite is true. Too many people who are suffering, not knowing what else to do and afraid of the answers others might give, merely react to their pain by throwing away careers, families, and beliefs, only to end up in similar, unhappy circumstances with a new job, marriage, or worldview. At that point they decide that life is simply too complicated for them and that their expectations from life are simply too high.

Sometimes it is important to make a radical change in your life, to shake things up, as it were. But how do you know whether the frustration and disappointment you are encountering requires a minor attitude adjustment—or a major life overhaul?

Horses or Zebras?

I am told that in medical school, students are taught to "look for horses before zebras." In other words, they must always rule out the most likely explanations for the problem before searching for more exotic answers. This approach prevents the patient from undergoing unnecessary tests and the doctor from prescribing more radical treatments than necessary.

When we are confronting the pain of our disappointments, it is very easy to chase zebras. We think what is missing is the exotic, the novel. We despise what we know, and long for the excitement that will come from being "over there."

es—in fact, too often—we leave everything
to go "over there," only to discover that we have
brought to this new place the same things that made us
miserable in the old place. The same crummy attitude, the
same erroneous beliefs, the same ridiculous expectations, and
the same personal limitations continue to haunt us; only the
scenery has changed. Once the novelty wears off, we realize
that zebras are really just horses with stripes, and we become
bored and disillusioned all over again.

When you reach this point, you're in danger of repeating
your futile search. What animal will you chase now? Whom
will you leave in your wake this time? When will it end?

The eminent psychologist Martin Seligman made a study
of happiness, reported in his book, *Authentic Happiness* (Free
Press, 2002). What makes some people happy and others
miserable? This highly respected study drove home the point
that happiness is not based on circumstance. According to a
Newsweek magazine article on Seligman's findings, "Health,
wealth, good looks, and status have astonishingly little effect
on what researchers call 'subjective well-being.' Even
paraplegics and lottery winners return to their [contentment]
baseline once they've had six months to adjust to their sudden
change of fortune."

Fulfillment, then, is less dependent upon changing your
circumstances than it is dependent upon changing yourself.
To prevent yourself from responding to the disappointment
and frustration in your life in a ham-fisted, reactionary, zebra-
hunting manner, the first question you have to ask yourself is
this: "Am I feeling unfulfilled because I am doing the wrong
thing with my life, or is the *real* problem that I am
approaching the life I have in a way that causes me to be
deathly bored with it?"

This is an extremely important question. Too many people think that they are wasting their time doing the wrong thing with the wrong people, when in fact, they are exactly where they ought to be—only the novelty has worn off.

It is time that we faced the truth about ourselves. We in the prosperous West are a fickle people. We live in an entertainment-oriented, amusement-based, disposable culture. As children we are catechized in the toy room, where we learn that the answer to boredom is novelty: Out with the old (defined in minutes, not years) and in with the new. This lesson becomes easily and deeply ingrained in each of us. Then, in adulthood, we try to apply what we have learned every time we find ourselves saying, "I think I need a change."

We are all familiar with the saying that "familiarity breeds contempt." But the truth is that boredom does not come primarily from the lack of new and novel experiences with which to amuse ourselves. It comes from our refusal to pursue meaning, virtue, and intimacy in the circumstances in which we find ourselves.

The teenager sitting around whining "I'm bored" isn't exploring new ways to use her gifts more fully. She is not attempting to build stronger and more intimate relationships with the people around her. And she is certainly not attempting to increase in her capacity for virtue. In fact, she is probably doing the opposite of all three.

Instead of exercising her many gifts, she is passively sitting on her tuffet waiting to be amused. She is probably doing all she can to avoid her stupid parents and her obnoxious siblings. Last but certainly not least important, she is hardly concerning herself with expanding her capacity for virtue, looking for new ways to be a better servant to those she meets.

No, the little princess is *bored*. Good heavens! Alert the press! The kingdom is in crisis.

Perhaps I am being a bit harsh. Perhaps not. I would be the first to tell you that if I added up all the hours I sat around whining about being bored or chasing after the next big thing that would make me happy, and subtracted that number from my age, I would probably be half as old as I am now. Would that I could get that time back. Would that I had never wasted it in the first place.

I am not denying that you may need a radical change in your life. In fact, if you determine that such a change is necessary, the remaining chapters in this book will describe how to identify the nature of that change, how to devise a practical plan, and how to get out of your own way so that you can fulfill that plan. Yet, for the moment, I will ask you to indulge me.

Just for the sake of argument, I want you to stop dreaming about how wonderful it is in that exotically green field over there where the zebras run free and instead look around the field you are in right now, checking to make sure that you have a good dose of horse sense. Is the reason you are unfulfilled not that you haven't yet found the right place or people, but rather that you are refusing to rise to the challenge of mining meaning, intimacy, and virtue out of the circumstances and life you currently enjoy?

Let's take a moment to find out.

Meaning—Using the Gifts You've Been Given

Calvin does not enjoy his job. Every morning, he comes into the office as late as he can without attracting attention. He does his work adequately well and he usually receives good reviews of his work, but he does not attempt to bring any of his personality, style, or creativity to bear on what he does. Secretly, and sometimes not so secretly, he counts the minutes until the end of the day—not because there is something to be excited about doing when he leaves work, but because he is just glad to get out of there.

Calvin wishes that he could find something else to do, but when it comes right down to it, it's a paycheck, and he really doesn't need any more hassles than he already has.

* * *

Ginny knows that being a stay-at-home mom is important. After all, that's why she does it. But when it comes right down to it, she herself feels bored and unimportant much of the time.

Housekeeping is thankless work. Just when you finish it, you have to start over again. It just seems so pointless.

Of course, she loves her kids. But inside, she loves to get them out the door for school in the morning. And even though she misses them while they're gone, she gets a sinking feeling in her gut in the afternoon (though she would be horrified if anyone ever found out) just before she hears the school bus coming down the street.

Ginny becomes furious when her husband suggests it, yet she knows that she spends as much time as possible avoiding the work that is hers to do. Even though she is not keeping up with her tasks at home, she volunteers for as many committees in the church and community as she is able to serve—she feels appreciated there. She also spends a goodly portion of her day on the phone and the Internet, where many of her Facebook chats involve describing how thankless her life is, and how little time she has to get everything done.

* * *

You will recall from the last chapter that a sense of meaning comes from attempting to use fully the gifts you have been given for the good of others and the glory of God in whatever circumstances you find yourself. While certain activities may be more meaningful than others because they give you greater opportunity to use your gifts, all activities can be the source of a sense of meaningfulness—to one degree or another—if you are constantly striving to bring everything you have to the task at hand, whether that task is a job, role, or relationship. By contrast, a sense of boredom and meaninglessness comes when we hold back. Every time we merely act as if we are going through the motions, or we treat the work or relationships we have in too casual a manner, we rob a moment of its potential to be meaningful, and therefore to be a source of joy.

Meaningfulness Quiz

This quiz offers you an opportunity to take stock of how talented you are at drawing meaning out of your circumstances, whatever they are. Mark the following statements true or false. If you are unsure, give the answer that describes how you are most often.

___ I value the work I do or tasks that fill my day.

___ I *do not* spend my day trying to avoid the tasks that are an essential part of my work and roles.

___ I am constantly looking for new and better ways to apply my gifts to my work or the roles I play.

___ If I had to give account to him today, I believe God would be pleased with how I approach my present work or roles.

___ I actively seek out opportunities to learn more about performing my work and roles better and more creatively.

___ The people who are closest to me would say that my priorities are in order.

___ I know how to listen to God speaking to me through the simple activities and happenings of my daily life.

___ I *do not* pursue one aspect of my life, work, or roles to the exclusion or detriment of the others.

___ Daily, I pray that God would help me learn how to serve him better in the work and roles in which I am currently involved.

___ I feel a sense of accomplishment, *not* merely relief, when I complete even the mundane tasks that are essential to my work and roles.

Scoring: Give yourself one point for each statement you marked "true."

Your score is _____ out of 10.

9-10. You are very talented at drawing meaning out of your circumstances.

7-8. You are not as intentional about your life as you should be. Your priorities may be regularly called into question and you may have a tendency to indulge in escapism. Make it a point to ask yourself how to use your gifts more fully in the tasks you encounter throughout the day. Pray each day that God would teach you to be a more faithful, eager servant in the tasks you have been given so that one day, he might entrust you with more responsibility.

6 or less. You tend to place a high premium on escapism. Your priorities are most likely highly suspect. You may wish to seek professional help to assist you in clarifying your gifts and how to apply them consistently and effectively to your life. For one possible avenue, contact the Pastoral Solutions Institute to enquire about tele-counseling and other services that can help you live more meaningfully.

Living meaningfully is another way to say that we must, as St. Josemaria Escriva once wrote, "sanctify our everyday life." There is no task too menial or simple that it does not matter to God. Everything we do is potentially filled with meaning and presents an opportunity to grow in all the qualities that enable us to live life as a gift.

St. Catherine of Siena is a Doctor of the Church—a wise woman who, in addition to her many spiritual insights and ecstasies, was largely responsible for the papacy's return to Rome after having moved to Avignon for many years. But in his famous book *Introduction to the Devout Life,* St. Francis de Sales observed that the most inspiring thing about St. Catherine of Siena's life was not the profound intelligence of her writing or her spiritual ecstasies. It was the loving and devoted service she offered to her parents and many brothers and sisters. He wrote:

> I did not doubt that by the eye of contemplation she had ravished the heart of her heavenly spouse. But I was equally comforted when I saw her in her father's

kitchen, humbly turning the spit, kindling fires, dressing meat, kneading bread, and doing the meanest of household chores cheerfully and filled with love and affection for God. . . . Her manner of meditating was as follows. While preparing her father's food she imagined that like another Martha, she was preparing it for our Savior, and that her mother had the place of Our Lady, and her brothers, that of the apostles. In this way, she roused herself to serve in spirit the whole court of heaven while joyously carrying out these humble tasks because she knew that such was God's will.

Meaningfulness is not achieved by the greatness of our actions, but by the great degree of care, creativity, love, and spirituality we *bring to* those actions, no matter how simple or mundane.

Whatever our score on the "Meaningfulness Quiz," we can all benefit from trying to draw more meaning out of the present work we do and roles we fill. The following tips can help us approach our present life in a more rewarding, meaningful manner.

1. Bring each day before the Lord. Pray: *Lord, help me to draw meaning from my life. Give me the courage to rise to the challenges I will face today with grace. Help me to use my gifts fully in the work I do that I might glorify you and serve the people in my life as you would have me do.*

2. Fight through your sense of boredom. Look for new ways to do old tasks. Ask yourself, what gifts or qualities do I possess that I am not applying to this work or role? How could I more effectively apply those qualities today? Write your specific answers on the lines below.

---

3. Learn more about all the aspects of your work, *especially* the parts you find boring or uninteresting. The more you learn about a subject, the more competent you become, and the more competent you are at an activity, the more you tend to experience it as meaningful. You may never learn to be passionate about that thing you used to hate, but you may learn to enjoy parts of it or come to a greater appreciation of the necessity or importance of that work. How will you apply this principle to your life?

---

4. Think of a week when you had a better attitude about your work or role. What simple differences allowed you to feel more optimistic that week? Did you get more sleep? Reverse the order in which you usually do things? Do things differently somehow? Something was different, and that difference allowed you to feel more positive about this aspect of your life. If you can identify that difference, you can exploit it by conscientiously applying it to the task at hand, thus increasing the likelihood that you will have more weeks that are better. List those differences here.

---

5. If you are able to master the previous tip, keep your eyes open for weeks that are spontaneously better. Note these new differences and look for ways to exploit them in the future as well. This way, you can improve your sense of meaningfulness step-by-step over time. List those differences here.

_____

_____

_____

I do not intend to imply that meaningfulness can be yours in five easy steps. But you can begin experiencing a greater sense of meaning in your life if you start applying the principles I outline above.

When I make these suggestions to people, the most common resistance I encounter is the fear that if they somehow decrease their hatred of a particular activity, work, or role, then they will be doomed to keep doing that for the rest of their natural life. Somehow, we think that if we simply refuse to do anything to relieve our distaste for an activity, God will deliver us from it, but if we actually rise to the challenge, God will think we don't need the help and leave us stuck in something we hate.

As creative as this thinking is, the only thing missing is the part where we tell God that we will hold our breath until we turn blue unless he gives us our way. The fact is, we cannot tantrum our way into the Lord's heart. Scripture tells us that it is the person who succeeds in lesser things who will be entrusted with greater things (see Lk 16:10). In a sense, if you wish God to give you a "promotion" out of the life you currently live, you will have to earn it by first performing well at the tasks you have been given.

Every kind of work we do, every role we play, every experience we encounter, no matter how silly or transitory it may seem, contains within it a lesson that we must learn before we can advance to the next step of the plan God has for our lives. Some of those steps are small, some large. But when we submit ourselves to the task at hand and learn to be a good servant to God in the particular work we have been given, we actually hasten the process by which we can be entrusted with greater opportunities for meaningfulness, intimacy, and virtue.

Unfortunately, because this work is harder in the short run, though infinitely more fulfilling in the long run, most people pursue immediate comfort instead of ultimate meaning and fulfillment. This valuing of comfort at the expense of meaning, intimacy, and virtue is known as *sloth,* one of the so-called seven deadly sins. In particular, the vice of sloth is deadly because it inhibits growth, actualization, and sanctification.

Life for the slothful person does not become more abundant with time. It either remains the same or lessens. Those who choose comfort over doing the comparatively more difficult work of pursuing meaning never get to where they are going because their lives are a series of lateral moves.

If they are unwilling to do the work necessary to pursue deeper meaning, they can go only so far before running headfirst into a very high, very thick wall. But instead of learning to scale that wall, the slothful tell themselves that the secret to happiness is to have as many experiences as possible while walking along the length of the wall. So they never get to see the whole new world on the other side of the wall.

Eventually, the restlessness that accompanies this lateral journey will translate into an alienation from the self and others that ultimately leads to a sense of disaffection, disappointment, and frustration with life. These individuals may consider themselves highly spiritual, but they actually lack any true sense of direction, purpose, or joy. Instead, they go from experience to experience, sensation to sensation, relationship to relationship, trying to fill the void that grows within.

Nevertheless, as St. Augustine observed, the heart is restless until it comes to rest in God. Constantly, God calls out to us and invites us to pursue the meaningfulness that is packed into every experience of life. By practicing the five tips outlined earlier in this section, our life can become more fertile by virtue of grace, bringing forth all manner of new experiences for meaning, intimacy, virtue, and the resultant joy.

Now let's examine the second quality: *intimacy*.

Intimacy: Vulnerability for the Sake of Love

Robert, forty-seven, has been married to Jenna for twenty years. He prides himself on the fact that in all that time, he has not changed a bit.

"I am who I am," Robert declared emphatically. "But Jenna keeps pestering me: 'I want you to open up. I want you to share more with me.' I don't know what more she wants. I'm giving her what I have to give. I wish she would just get off my back and accept me for who I am."

I asked Robert to tell me who he was exactly. He answered, "Oh, you know. I guess I'm pretty self-sufficient. I don't need much from other people. That's what Jenna wants me to be, more needy, I guess, but I don't think it's good to be too needy."

I asked him why not. "Oh, I don't know. It's better just to handle things yourself so no one lets you down."

* * *

Allison, forty-three, was depressed and anxious. Married ten years, she confessed that she felt suffocated in the relationship.

"It's not like he's controlling or anything," she admits. "I can do what I like. But it's just that he wants more from me than I can give, y'know?"

I asked her to explain what she meant.

"He's just real lovey, and I'm just not that way. He is always telling me that he loves me and wants to hold hands and spend time together. I tell him that I have too much to do.

"Don't get me wrong. I'm glad that he loves me, but it just seems like after ten years of marriage maybe we could be over the honeymoon stage and just be a little more practical. We have kids. We're both busy people.

"Frankly, as far as I'm concerned, I don't think he understands that I just want space. I'm not comfortable being affectionate or demonstrative. My family wasn't that way at all, and I don't quite know what to do with it."

* * *

Intimacy is the willingness to make ourselves vulnerable for the sake of love. As I explain in my book *For Better . . . FOREVER!*, intimacy is to love what a depth gauge is to water.

In other words, someone may love us, but their capacity for intimacy tells us whether we will ultimately experience that love as a puddle or an ocean. Intimacy compels us to foster a greater capacity for emotional, verbal, and physical communication. It challenges us to seek the truth, goodness, and beauty in the things that the person with whom we seek intimacy also experiences as true, good, and beautiful.

In a sense, intimacy is the fruit of a special kind of love the Church calls *self-donation:* that willingness to use my whole self—body, mind, and spirit—to work for the good of another. Whether we are talking about a husband and wife, a parent and child, or two close friends, when two people practice this kind of self-donative love for each other, a deep bond is formed.

Contrary to popular belief, we do not exist as individuals, single, self-contained atomic units that occasionally bump into each other. Rather, the Church tells us that all people are, by virtue of their being, an integral part of the "intimate community of persons." People often mention the phrase "social system," but they rarely understand the significance of that statement. The fact is, to be human is to be social, not in some metaphorical "isn't it lovely to have company around now and then" sense, but in the same sense that being human means having skin, organs, and a nervous system.

In other words, the social system is as much an actual part of the human person as the digestive system, the respiratory system, the nervous system, and so on. As physiological proof of this, babies will reject even food and liquid if they are deprived of the comforting touch of another person. Likewise, neuroscientists are discovering the incredibly interpersonal nature of the brain. Many recent studies have shown that intimate, affectionate relationships actually wire the part of the brain known as "the center of free will" (the orbito-frontal cortex), which is much more highly developed in people who actively work to build intimacy in their lives.

Likewise, the capacity a person exhibits for intimate relationships with others is a standard hallmark of that person's mental health. We'll discuss much of this more thoroughly in the chapter on changing your life in a manner that is respectful of others, but for now, it is important to simply know that intimacy is a good indicator of the condition of a person's humanity.

Intimacy Quiz

How great is your capacity for intimacy? Take this quiz. Mark the following statements true or false.

___ I am comfortable sharing my hopes, dreams, and fears with those who are close to me.

___ My spouse and children (or if I am unmarried, the people who are closest to me) would say that I love them well.

___ I am *not* ashamed to be vulnerable in front of others—that is, to receive charitable correction, to be told that I am wrong, or to make a fool of myself sometimes.

___ I do *not* become defensive easily.

___ Each day, I look for ways to make the lives of those people who are closest to me (especially a spouse or children) easier or more pleasant.

___ I enjoy and actively seek out the company of those I am closest to (especially, if married, the company of my spouse and children).

___ I am comfortable with and thoroughly enjoy physical displays of affection.

___ The people who are closest to me would say that they enjoy confiding in me because I am a sensitive and loving listener.

___ Though I do not seek it out unnecessarily, I am not intimidated by conflict.

___ I am an effective communicator and listener.

___ I work hard to accommodate the requests of those closest to me—even the requests that challenge me or make me uncomfortable—as long as a request is not demeaning or morally offensive.

___ Even when I don't enjoy or understand it, I go out of my way to share in and be knowledgeable about the activities or interests the people closest to me enjoy (for example, their hobbies, interests, passions, work, spirituality).

Scoring: Give yourself one point for each statement you marked "true."

Your score is _____ out of 12.

11-12. You have an exceptional capacity for intimacy. You experience your relationships as rewarding; you are adept at handling conflict and comfortable being vulnerable around others, though you are able to avoid the extremes of appearing to be either a doormat or a tank. Others find you to be a good and caring confidant, and they value your company.

8-10. You have a fair capacity for intimacy. You may, however, have a tendency to love people only to the degree that you are comfortable loving them—not necessarily as much as they need to be loved or in the way they need to be loved. Likewise, you may become more defensive than is helpful in the face of even charitable criticism, which makes others shy away from sharing hard truths about you or themselves.

You need to work on finding healthy ways to challenge your comfort zone and learn to be more vulnerable and present with others. For additional tips to improve your "intimacy quotient," see Daniel Goleman, *Emotional Intelligence*; and my books *For Better . . . FOREVER! A Catholic Guide to Lifelong Marriage* and *The Exceptional Seven Percent: Nine Secrets of the World's Happiest Couples*.

7 or less. You have a poor capacity for intimacy. You may tend to think of yourself as loving, but it probably means to you something different from what it means to the people around you who often do not feel well cared for by you. You become hostile when challenged—even charitably—by those who are close to you.

You have a tendency to value accomplishments over relationships and may tend to pride yourself on how little you need others. You wish they could be more like you and just "get off your back." Your pride, however, is just a smoke screen that hides an impoverished life and psyche.

You will need to increase your sensitivity to others and decrease your addiction to your own comfort and validation. In addition to the books mentioned above, you may wish to seek professional assistance to guide you through the defenses you use to keep yourself aloof from others. Call the Pastoral Solutions Institute at for more information.

Increasing Your Intimacy Quotient

If intimacy is so desirable and so essential for joy and living abundantly, why do so many of us waste so much time avoiding it? One of the reasons we have already noted: sloth, that preference for our own comfort over the significantly more difficult activity of learning how to love and be loved. But I believe that another factor is involved as well: *pride*.

Most of us know that we aren't perfect. But those who struggle with pride attempt to hide from others—to the point of apparent obliteration—their incompleteness. The typical result is people who may seem to have many friends, but whom no one really knows. Alternatively, they are people who, though miserable, defensive, aloof, and sullen, insist on denying that they have a problem.

In both cases, the proud are really more like a rotten egg than a human being: On the outside, they are a clean, hard shell presenting a smooth face to the world. But hidden within lies a mess that even they themselves don't wish to confront.

What the proud person forgets, of course, is that relationships are not for the perfect. Rather, relationships are the catalyst that moves us toward perfection. When we are willing to expose our brokenness to someone who loves us, we enable that relationship to become an instrument of transforming grace.

* * *

Len, forty-eight, was married to Carryl, forty-six. Though well liked by many people at the office, Len had few if any real friends. He and his wife had endured a conflicted relationship for many years. Often, Len's behavior toward Carryl was verbally abusive. He responded to even gentle suggestions with hostility and insisted: "Either she takes me as I am, or I go."

Carryl called me, desperate. She couldn't stand living with him anymore, even though she said she loved him and didn't want to leave. Working individually with Carryl at first, I was able to help her find some ways to crack Len's armor safely.

One Sunday they had a huge fight about the budget. Using techniques we had discussed in session, Carryl was able to remain calm but forceful. When Len blew up, he usually found some way to blame her for his outburst, but not this time. She remained composed and focused on her goal: getting him to apologize sincerely for his behavior and agree to get treatment for it.

Her calm demeanor forced Len to confront the fact that his own behavior was childish and irrational. Carryl's charitably firm persistence finally motivated Len to contact me for counseling as well. Through our work, Len was able to confront his fear of being found out as imperfect, to admit his mistakes readily, to take criticism well, and to respond charitably when he felt attacked. His transformation was remarkable, really. But it all started when he was willing to overcome his pride.

Len explained it this way in one of our final sessions: "I was so afraid she would find out how messed up my head really was. When we had that argument, though, I finally saw what a jerk I was being, and I was forced to apologize— sincerely— maybe for the first time in my life. It was the first time I let Carryl get a foot in the door of my life in nearly twenty years of marriage.

"Looking back, I can't believe how much time I wasted. I should have done this years ago. Once I got over myself and trying to pretend that I didn't have any problems—it was really her fault, I thought—I could see that she would still love me even if I wasn't perfect I know that it was stupid. But since I actually let her in, I feel closer to her than I ever have."

Carryl agreed. 1 feel like he's finally letting me get to know him. I always knew he loved me, but he just didn't love me enough to let me know him. Lately, it's been better than ever."

* * *

Carryl and Len's story is a good example of what can happen when we overcome our addiction to our own personal comfort and our pride. Of course, to varying degrees, sloth and pride affect us all and stand in the way of our ability to form truly intimate relationships. That's tragic.

I say this because heaven is nothing more than being in the complete and overwhelmingly intimate presence of God. If we cannot achieve intimacy with our spouse, our children, or at least a handful of close, loving friends, how can we ever hope to tolerate, much less appreciate, an eternity of intimacy with the Source of all things intimate?

Living abundantly, and experiencing the joy that accompanies it, is directly dependent upon our capacity for intimacy. Regardless of your intimacy quotient, the following tips can help you supercharge your ability to love and be loved.

1. Each day, seek another, specific way to make the lives
    of those around you easier or more pleasant. Write
    some examples here.

    _____

    _____

    _____

    _____

    _____

2. Respond generously to all requests from those closest to
    you (especially a spouse and children), assuming that
    you do not experience those requests as demeaning or
    morally offensive. This rule of thumb stands at the
    heart of the kind of generous love that fuels true
    intimacy. What requests have you been avoiding but
    could fulfill if you were simply willing to challenge
    your comfort zone? Write your answers here.

    _____

    _____

    _____

3. Overcome your fear of saying hard truths charitably
    and hearing charitably spoken hard truths about
    yourself. No one likes conflict or enjoys being
    criticized, even charitably. As the Scripture says,
    "For the moment all discipline seems painful rather
    than pleasant." But Scripture also tells us that later
    on, such measures produce "the peaceful fruit of
    righteousness" (Heb 12:11).

    Scripture might just as well include intimacy on that
    list. When people speak the truth in love, they play a
    role in helping each other become the people God
    created them to be. When you can look at someone and
    say, "I am a better person today than I was before, and

I have you to thank for that," then you know the power and joy of an intimate relationship.

What shortcomings have others pointed out to you that you have previously been defensive about? List those shortcomings, and some ideas for changing them, here.

_____

_____

_____

_____

4. Be affectionate. Many people are restrained in the physical and verbal affection they offer to one another. Instead of reaching out and using our bodies, minds, and spirits to work for the good of others, we hold back, saying, "It makes me uncomfortable."

But we were made to express affection abundantly, just as our heavenly Father displays his love passionately and fully. We need to recognize that refusing to offer affection to another because "we are just not that way" is a lie. We *are* that way.

To be human is to be affectionate. As we saw, babies will die if they are not given affection. The need to give and receive affection is hardwired into each human being by God. If affection makes you uncomfortable, then you need to recognize that this is because, at some point in your life, this natural, God-given desire was trained out of you.

Your joy, indeed, your sanctification (which is nothing if it is not the process by which we make ourselves ready for an intimate relationship with God and the communion of saints) depends on your deepening your capacity for intimacy. So challenge the

sloth that compels you to prefer your comfort over
your call to love. Seek help if you need to grow in this
area and cannot do it on your own.

What are the ways in which others have asked you
to be more affectionate but you have resisted? List
them here, along with what you plan to do to respond
more generously in the future.

_____

_____

_____

_____

5. Seek the truth, goodness, and beauty in the things
   those closest to you find true, good, and beautiful.
   Think about it: We are closest to the people who share
   our interests and competencies. So if you desire greater
   intimacy in your life, you must be willing to stretch
   yourself to participate in (or at least be knowledgeable
   about) those things that the people closest to you find
   true, good, and beautiful. (This excludes, of course,
   those activities that are morally offensive or personally
   demeaning.)

   Too often, we build walls to intimacy by turning
   down the invitations we are given to share another's joy.
   "Oh, no thanks. You know I don't like that; just do that
   with your other friends." This phrase, though innocent
   enough, is another example of how we choose our own
   comfort over love, actualization, and sanctification.

If we want to live a joyful, abundant, intimate life, we
must tear down the altar we have built to maintaining our
comfort and be willing instead to stretch in this way. When
we do, we respond to the voice of God calling us to come out

of our own little worlds and build community with others. When we do this, we have more to share with those around us, and based on these mutual experiences, we open up to one another more fully.

Imagine if you were able to apply thoroughly the tips listed above. What would your life be like? Surely, it would be hard work, but if the payoff were deeper, more committed, engaging, intimate relationships, wouldn't it be worth the work?

Having looked at the second ingredient of abundant living, let's examine the last essential ingredient: *virtue*.

Virtue—The Key to Joy

A few years back I wrote a book about marriage whose content is completely consistent with Catholic teaching, yet whose intended audience is largely secular; the text has no theological references at all. Throughout its pages, I demonstrate that those couples who have the happiest relationships take the pursuit of virtues such as love, service, joy, intimacy, communication, gratitude, growth, and generosity very seriously.

Interestingly enough, my editor, in offering her feedback on the finished manuscript, raised an objection. She commented: "It's like you're asking people to become saints!"

The forceful and shocked manner in which she expressed her disbelief stunned me into silence for a moment. When my capacity for speech returned, I found myself saying, "And the problem with that is . . . ?"

We tend to think of virtue as a list of things that holy people in far-off places do because—if we must be completely honest about it—they are not quite right in the head. This is nonsense. Though we are dealing with it last in our list of three essentials, virtue is nevertheless the key to an abundant life. It is the key to true joy.

I know, I know—that sounds awfully dull, but you need to trust me a little bit. Virtue really is the key to finding the kind of happiness, intimacy, and meaning that you have been craving.

Heaven is being in the presence of God, and we all know that heaven is a place of unending joy and abundant life, right? Well, God manifests his presence in this world through virtue. Every time we choose love, justice, wisdom, self-control, or any other virtue over our mere comfort or preference, God himself enters into *our* lives more fully. The more God is present in our lives and relationships, the more we are able to experience the joy that accompanies creating heaven on Earth.

Virtue Quiz

How much does virtue play a role in your life? Obviously, we cannot offer a tool for making a comprehensive examination of virtue in your life in so small a space, but this quiz will address your overall attitude toward the pursuit of virtue in general.

Rate yourself on a scale of 1-3.

1 = "Mostly False"; 2 = "Somewhat True";
3 = "Mostly True"

___ Daily, I bring my relationships to the Lord and ask him to give me the wisdom and charity I need to be a good servant to the people in my life.

___ I *always* ask God to give me his wisdom before I make even small decisions about my work or life.

— I am able to say what needs to be said and say it *charitably*.

— I am able to speak the truth even when it means other people may be upset with me.

— I *do not* become defensive or hostile when someone points out how I have hurt them.

— A stranger could tell what spiritual and moral values are really important to me merely by witnessing the choices I make, the priorities I set, and the depth and health of my relationships.

— Every day, I could name at least one specific thing I have done *intentionally* to make the lives of those around me easier or more pleasant.

— The people who know me best (such as spouse and children) would say that I am a good and positive example to others.

— I know how to balance my work effectively with the needs of those who count on me.

— I work very hard to overcome laziness, my own preferences, tiredness, or even—when possible—sickness, to make myself available to meet the needs of those who count on me.

— I have good self-control.

— I bear wrongs patiently and am quick to forgive.

— My feelings do *not* rule me. I am in charge of my emotional life.

— I am able to resist the temptation to indulge my own comfort at the expense of my beliefs and those who count on me.

— Those who count on me would say that I inspire their trust, love, and confidence.

Scoring: Tally up your points.

You received _____ out of a possible 45 points.

40-45. Your life reflects a very active pursuit of virtue. In spite of your weaknesses and failings, you daily strive to be the best person you can be. Keep working to expand your capacity for service and love.

35-39. You are fairly conscientious about applying virtue to your life and relationships. Follow the tips in this chapter to make you more aware of how you can live your Christian mission more fully, especially in your intimate relationships.

34 or less. While virtue is important to you as a concept, you are not as intentional about living it out in your daily life as you need to be. Follow the tips in this chapter to increase your awareness of becoming more intentional about pursuing virtue in your life. You may wish to seek counseling or spiritual direction to assist you in maintaining the accountability you may need to be more faithful to your beliefs and values.

Consciously applying virtues such as faith, hope, love, prudence, temperance, justice, fortitude, patience, kindness, and self-control to our discussions and interactions enables our whole life to become a prayer.

A Living Prayer

People constantly complain that they do not have time to pray. But when you consciously attempt to live out the virtues that are key to the Christian walk, every action becomes a living prayer. To pray is to invite God into your daily life and interactions. So when you get off the couch and serve your family even when you're tired, or when you play a game with your children that you frankly think is silly, or when you do anything that places your pursuit of virtue over comfort, you invite God more fully into your life and relationships—and the action that inspires this invitation is, in fact, a form of prayer.

Though people complain about not having time to pray, they tell me that they derive a great deal of peace and joy from the experience of prayer. Imagine if you could carry that sense of peace and joy with you all day long. I don't mean an artificial peace that allows you to float above all the events of everyday life, but a real peace and joy that allow you to know that you have what it takes (that is, God) to be victorious no matter what life throws at you.

This is one of the fruits of living a virtuous life. Suddenly it doesn't sound quite so boring and unattractive, does it? Challenging? Perhaps. Boring and dull? Never. By inviting God more fully into your life, not just with words but with your virtuous actions, God, the author of meaning and intimacy, will show you—step-by-step—how to find both of these, and with them comes the joy of living abundantly.

The development of virtue and the effects that this pursuit has on relationships is a major theme in my work. In many of my books, I give extensive exercises for applying virtue to parenting, marital, and other personal relationships. I do not wish to be redundant here, so I will give you only a basic outline of the process.

Step One

Prayerfully consider the major virtues and qualities of the Christian walk as they appear in the following list. Obviously you want to possess all of these, but there are probably two or three that would be especially useful to you at this time in your life. Identify those virtues that God is calling you to emphasize in your present circumstances.

The Theological Virtues: faith, hope, charity. *The Cardinal Virtues:* prudence, justice, temperance, fortitude (courage).

The Fruit of the Spirit (see Gal 5:22-23): love, joy, peace, patience, kindness, goodness, faithfulness, gentleness, self-control. *Other Qualities:* chastity, modesty, hospitality, openness, creativity, respect . . .

List others here:

_____

_____

_____

_____

Considering these examples of virtues and other desirable qualities, which do you feel called to emphasize in your life at this time?

_____

_____

_____

_____

Step Two

Ask yourself, "If I lived out these qualities more fully in my life, what specific things would I need to do differently?" For example: "If I wanted to be more loving, I would need to respond differently when my spouse says such and such." Or, "If I wanted to be more generous, I would offer to do thus and such more often without being asked."

What would you need to do?

_____

_____

_____

_____

Step Three

Pray and continually evaluate. Each day, ask God to give you the strength to be faithful to these goals. Further, ask God to help your life become a living prayer so that you can see how even the smallest actions offer the greatest opportunity for spiritual growth.

On the days you struggle, make specific plans about how you will do better tomorrow. When these behaviors become second nature to you, reassess the list of virtues and ask yourself what you should work on next. In this way, you will be constantly striving to be a better servant to God and those around you, and you will increase the intimacy, meaning, and joy you experience in your life and relationships.

For more information about filling out the brief strategy outline above, check out the books I've previously noted: *The Exceptional Seven Percent: Nine Secrets of the World's Happiest Couples; For Better . . . FOREVER! A Catholic Guide to Lifelong Marriage;* and *Parenting With Grace: The Catholic Parent's Guide to Raising (Almost) Perfect Kids.*

Bringing It All Together

In this chapter, we have attempted to assess whether you are unhappy because you need a major change in your life or rather because you are simply not living fully in the life you have already been given. Before we close out this chapter, I want to pull it all together for you. Go back through the quizzes you have taken. Write the scores you received for each in the spaces provided.

    Meaningfulness Quiz _____
    Intimacy Quiz   _____
    Virtue Quiz   _____

Now, add these three scores to arrive at your total score for the chapter.
Total Score: _____ out of a possible 67 points.

This total score represents how abundantly you are living the life you currently have.

60-67. You are doing everything you can to live the fullest life possible in your present circumstances. If you feel unfulfilled in spite of your efforts, it is probably time to make a change. The dissatisfaction you feel may be the Holy Spirit calling you to move on to the next stage of your life. To discern what that next stage is, follow the tips presented throughout the rest of the book.

50-59. You are not making the most of the opportunities God is giving you to live an abundant life in your present circumstances. While it may be necessary to make more significant changes in your life, it would be most appropriate to work first on learning how to approach the life you already have in a more meaningful, intimate, and virtuous manner. If you do not, then it is likely that your future will not be any more rewarding than your present once the novelty of change wears off. Use the tips throughout this book to discern where God is leading you next, but do not forget to live fully now.

49 or less. You are not making enough of an effort to live abundantly in the present. Unless you work first on increasing your capacity for, and experience of, meaningfulness, intimacy, and virtue in your present circumstances, you will most likely not find happiness no matter what other changes you make in your life. These limitations will follow you wherever you go.

Happiness and fulfillment can be yours, but they must first come from within. I would not recommend making any significant changes in your circumstances until you have done serious work on these three areas first. Seek the help of a faithful counselor or a mature spiritual director to help you begin walking down the path of true abundance.

Having assessed your capacity for living fully regardless of your circumstances, we are now ready to examine questions such as these: How do you know what *God* wants you to do with your life? What is God leading you toward? How can you overcome the internal and external obstacles that stand between the life you have today and the life God is calling you to live?

To examine these questions, each of the following chapters will address in depth one of the following letters of the acronym FAITH that we noted in chapter one:

> **Follow** the Rules for Healthy Discernment.
> **Act,** Even When You Doubt.
> **Investigate** the Causes of Your Anxiety.
> **Take** Others into Account.
> **Hold On** Through Adversity.

Through the insights in these chapters, you will learn how to carry the lessons of abundant living with you so that wherever the road God asks you to walk may lead, you will be able to experience the joy that comes from always pursuing meaningfulness, intimacy, and virtue.

PART TWO
WALKING IN
F.A.I.T.H.

THREE

Follow the Rules for
Healthy Discernment

Aaron, thirty-eight, is at a loss. "How do I know what God wants me to do?" he asks. "I'm afraid that many of the things I want to do would jeopardize my family. At the same time, I don't think I can keep going the way I am. I feel so empty, but I feel paralyzed, too."

* * *

Rebecca, forty-three, feels frustrated in her marriage. Her husband is a workaholic who is rarely at home. She is alone with their four children most of the time. When he is home, he is often dismissive of her needs. She says, "Some days I feel like God is telling me I should stick it out; other days I feel like maybe he's telling me I should leave; and other days," she adds wryly, "I feel like maybe he's telling me that I can't trust my feelings."

* * *

In the first chapter, we saw that God desires our happiness, and we examined the three goals that we must seek to pursue true joy: greater meaning, intimacy, and godly virtue in life.

But how do you know what that means in your unique circumstances? What is meaningful to one person might be meaningless to another, what inspires intimacy in one person might be repulsive to a second, and what is virtuous in one set of circumstances might actually be a vice in a different context. How do you know what God wants you to do?

Confronting the unfulfilled expectations of life in a faithful way is different from confronting them without God. In the absence of God, the best we can do in the face of our disappointments is shrug and say, *"C'est la vie!"* ('That's life!") But the Christian is empowered to do better.

Imagine a child who orders a toy from a catalog. He waits and waits until finally, his package arrives. Excitedly, he tears open the box and takes out his prize, only to find that it's broken.

Many of us can relate to this sadness. We spend our youth imagining how it will be when we grow up. Then the package arrives, and we begin to wonder whom we can sue for false advertising.

But there is more to the story. Imagine that the child tearfully takes this toy to his loving father. The father scoops the child up into his lap and places the contents of the box on the table in front of him. Step-by-step, the father talks the child through the process of putting the pieces together.

At first, the child wishes that the father would just do it for him. He whines that it "isn't fair." He says that he wants to go play and that the father should just call him when it's finished.

But this father truly does know best. He wants his son to learn how to put the pieces together himself, but not because the father is lazy or doesn't care. In fact, the opposite is true. One day, the father wants the son to be a partner in the family business, and his son will have to be able to use his intellect and many other skills to become the partner the father wants him to be.

The father knows that if he just does the work for his son, his son will never be an effective partner. The son will always be weak and dependent. And so, step-by-step, the loving father not only teaches the child how to reassemble the toy, but also helps the child discover his inner gifts—all the skills that the child will need as he grows into manhood, until one day, the child will be able to inherit responsibly all that the father has to give.

And so it is with us. Without our loving Father, our situation is hopeless. We don't know how to put the pieces of our life together on our own. The best we can do is shrug, or cry, or moan, until finally we accept that this is just the way life is.

As a Christian, however, you are blessed beyond the fatherless child's wildest dreams. You have a heavenly Father who loves you more than you could ever know. He created you with your happiness in mind, and he holds the secrets to your abundant life in his heart. If you will bring the shattered pieces of your dreams to him, step-by-step he will show you how to assemble them, until all at once, you can look up at the work, amazed at the wonderful things your hands have accomplished, and be filled with gratitude for your Father who guided you every minute of the way.

When We Give Our Lives to God

All day long I confront hopelessness in my practice. So many people think that it is too late for them. They think that theirs is the unique life that is so disordered, so hopelessly broken, whose dreams are so terminally dead on arrival, that they cannot possibly be resuscitated, much less revitalized. But I want to assure you that nothing, *nothing,* is impossible with God (see Lk 1:37)—not even you.

When we give our lives to him, however incompletely, however imperfectly, he begins to work. A jackass in the wild goes where he will, and no master will guide him. But once even the most stubborn jackass (like me, for instance) finds a master, that master will lead him on the safest path.

The jackass may fight, kick, resist, and even break away. But once the poor, ignorant creature has found a master, that master will not fail him. He will comfort the beast when he becomes afraid, give him a shove when he is too stubborn, and bring him home when he has run away.

The same is true of each one of us. No matter how far we have managed to run away from the place God intended us to be. No matter how stubborn and fearful we are. No matter how lost and hopeless we think we are.

Once we have said, "Lord, be my master," he takes our reins. He begins guiding us on the safest path back to the fields where he always intended us to graze. And while this journey is always quicker and more pleasant when we consciously cooperate with it, sometimes he does all this even without our knowing it.

Both I and my clients—some of whose lives would appear to be hopelessly lost and unredeemable at first glance—never fail to be amazed at the power of God to take the most unfulfilled, shattered life and transform it into the envy of all. We shouldn't be surprised, of course: This is, after all, the God who takes lowly jackasses like you and me and leads us to the green pastures where he "spreads a banquet before us in the sight of all our foes" (see Ps 23:5).

Before we go any further, I want to challenge you to trust in the Lord. Pray these words: "Lord, be my master. Lead me. Guide me. Be my champion." You may be surprised that, by his grace, you are already further down the road than you expected to be.

Now let's talk about what it takes to cooperate more consciously with the Master who is trying to lead us.

Discerning His Will

One of the questions I am asked most frequently is: "How do I get from where I am to where God wants me to be?" To answer this question, we need to know three things.

1. Am I being tempted to pursue an option that violates God's laws?
2. What are the gifts God has given me, and how can I use them to work for the good of others?
3. How can I pursue those gifts more fully in a manner that is respectful of the people he has placed in my life?

Each of these questions contains an important piece of the jigsaw puzzle that is our life. To begin putting those pieces together, we need to reckon with all three of the above questions. Let's examine each.

1. *Am I being tempted to pursue an option that violates God's laws?*

This is an important first question to ask. Too often when we are frustrated and pained by the broken dreams that litter our lives, we would be willing to do anything to make us feel better.

* * *

Carl was miserable in his marriage for a long time. He was never very good with conflict, and so there were many years of resentments built up toward his wife. He became withdrawn from her and felt depressed much of the time.

He began working with a woman who was also going through tough times in her marriage. They began by offering support to each other, but their friendship quickly began to take on romantic overtones. Soon, Carl was involved in a full-blown affair.

In explaining the situation to me, he said, "I believe that God wants me to be happy, and this relationship is making me happier than I have been in years. I know that people would say I'm committing adultery, but I don't think so. I really think that God led me into this relationship."

I can tell you with certainty that God did not lead Carl to commit adultery. God may ask us to do many things, but he will never ask us to do anything that violates his commandments or the revealed truths we can find in the teachings of his Church (such as we find in the *Catechism)*.

Too often we think of the laws of God, the commandments, the beatitudes, and the teachings of the *Catechism* as repressive laws promulgated by a Church that has nothing better to do than complicate our lives. This may be the view the world takes toward the teachings of God and his Church, but that view is not shared by the faithful.

Part of the problem is that we are confronted by arbitrary and sometimes unjust human laws every day. One state says we can drive only fifty-five miles per hour, while another says we can drive seventy-five, and the only difference is that someone capriciously decided it should be so. A working-class family may pay more taxes proportionately than a rich family because they have fewer loopholes to exploit. If two people commit murder, the one with the bigger bank account and the better lawyer may get off, while the other spends the rest of his life in prison.

Because our human experience of laws is often more about legalities than justice, we tend to assume the same is true for the laws of God. We think that the commandments and the other teachings of God and his Church are "generally speaking, pretty good guidelines," but subject to change for individual extenuating circumstances. Yet that ignores an important fact.

God's laws do not change, because they are not about legalities. They are about justice. What's the difference? Law can be arbitrary, and it is often only tangentially concerned with the good of the individual. But justice is always about helping individuals do the right thing, resulting in an orderly and happy society. Divine justice is as much about pleasing God as it is about presenting the blueprint that will help us become the happy, fulfilled people he created us to be.

When we obey the speed limit, the government is happy, and we may or may not be the better for it. But when we obey the commandments of God and the teachings of the Church, we are not merely pleasing God and the Church hierarchy. We are following the plan that will ultimately lead to our happiness and fulfillment.

Remember, in the last chapter, I asserted that joy comes from pursuing meaning, intimacy, and *virtue*. When we abandon the instructions for living an abundant life (the commandments of God and the teachings of his Church), we abandon virtue, and we jeopardize our own chances for joy and fulfillment. God, who in his mercy can write straight with crooked lines, may be able to make something good out of the mess we bring him. But he could do it infinitely faster and less painfully if we followed the instructions he has already given us in order to lead us to that abundant life.

As you consider the many choices that are, or soon will become, available to you for putting the pieces of your dreams together, I urge you to rule out automatically any of those options you know to be contrary to God's commandments or the teachings of the Church. The best those options can offer you is the "happiness" that a drunk feels just before he wraps his car around a telephone pole. Your joy, your fulfillment, is dependent upon your pursuit of virtue, which means actively rejecting any option that goes against what God or his Church says you shouldn't do.

2. What are the gifts God has given me?

Once we have ruled out directions that are not healthy for us, we need to start figuring out where we can go. To do this, we have to begin by considering our gifts.

There are two problems here. First, many people doubt that they have been given any gifts. They do not know themselves to be great singers, or actors, or to possess any other obvious talent. So they think that they have nothing to offer.

This way of thinking is entirely wrongheaded. To discover your gifts, I want you to ask yourself one question:

FOLLOW THE RULES FOR HEALTHY DISCERNMENT

"What are the activities that give me joy?" When you know the answer to that, then you know what your gifts are.

"But I like to watch TV all day long."

Um, that's not quite what I mean. Remember, in the first chapter, I made a distinction between joy and mere pleasure. Pleasure is a *momentary* state that comes from engaging in an activity that *may or may not be good for you*. On the other hand, true joy comes from those activities that cause you to experience greater meaning in your life, invite you into deeper relationships with others, or enable you to achieve greater virtue. None of those goals are accomplished by staring at the television.

When I ask you to think about what activities give you joy, I am asking you to think about those activities that make you feel more alive, that cause others to be drawn to you, that make you feel that you are becoming a better, more vital, more human person when you do them.

* * *

Veronica loves reading. She is passionate about good books. She recently started a book discussion group at her local library. The last book she read opened her eyes to new insights about life. She loves to discover new things about language and the ideas of others.

* * *

Barry enjoys working in the garden. He loves getting his fingers in the dirt and doesn't mind the hard work involved in tilling the soil or moving rocks to make new borders and features. In fact, he gets a kick out of it. Barry's neighbors often admire his efforts, and he enjoys giving them advice about their own gardens. Last fall, he helped his neighbor plan and plant a huge bulb garden. Next spring, he is looking into taking a master gardener's class at the Civic Horticultural Center.

* * *

In each of the above examples, you see how Veronica and Barry both apply themselves to things that give them real joy. Veronica feels more alive when she is reading a good book or learning something new. Her passions drive her to share this joy with others, and that draws people closer to her. As she reflects on what she has read, she learns about herself and her world, becoming more wise and thoughtful about the gift of life.

Barry, for his part, experiences life more fully when his hands are working hard preparing soil and planting things. His passion causes him to draw others to him as well and to seek relationships with like-minded people. In addition, he uses his gifts for the good of others when he generously offers help and advice to those who seek out his expertise.

What activities and pursuits give you this sense of joy? These are your gifts, and fulfillment lies in your pursuit of them. Take a moment to reflect on these things that give you joy—not just pleasure, but real joy. What are those activities that make you feel more alive, lead you into deeper relationships with others, and cause you to be a more generous, helpful, or creative person? List some examples here.

1. _____

2. _____

3. _____

Why Did God Give Me These Gifts?

Many people think that their gifts are given to them for themselves. They think of their passions as hobbies that they do only when they have the time and only for their own pleasure. They are wrong.

The Church tells us that God gives us our gifts so that they might be used to work for the good of others. Our fulfillment, our joy, comes not only from knowing what we like to do, but figuring out a way of doing that to enrich other people's lives. If I play piano even relatively well and I do it alone in my house, that gives me pleasure. But if I take that gift and share it with others—say, I play in church, or give concerts at the nursing home, or even play for my friends at dinner parties—I will experience a greater sense of fulfillment that comes from joy.

It has nothing to do with "showing off." It has everything to do with recognizing that God has given me whatever he has given me *to enjoy and to share*. The more I discover and share my gifts, the more I will experience fulfillment.

Too many people have little joy in their lives because they think their gifts are disposable. "I used to like that when I was a kid, but I had to give it up when I became a grown-up and had to deal with real life."

I have fought this attitude my entire life. In part, I thank the Holy Spirit for having come into my heart at an early age and protected me from the fallacy of always having to be "practical." But in no small part, I have to thank my parents, and especially my father, who pursued his dream of becoming a photographer and opening his own studio.

I grew up in a blue-collar town filled with good, salt-of-the-earth people. I have fond memories of the generosity and love exhibited by many of those who worked in the mills and the mines of southwestern Pennsylvania. Some of the people I knew there really loved their work. Their friends sometimes thought they were crazy, but they enjoyed going to the factory or the mine each day and working hard, using the gift of their bodies to dig coal or make steel. They felt productive and, because they were using their gifts for the good of others, they felt joy.

By and large, however, most people I knew were not like that. Good, loving, and generous as they were, many of those I grew up around were not joyful, and many of them discouraged us children from pursuing joy as well. From an early age, I remember my relatives urging me: "Forget about doing what makes you happy. That's kid stuff. You have to be practical. You've got to think about getting a good job." By this they meant working in the mill or factories that, at the time, provided the security, wage, and benefits for which they sold their happiness.

By God's grace, though, I always had a natural sense that I must use to the fullest the gifts that God gave me. That the only way I could be the person he created me to be was by doing the most with what I have been given, using those gifts to try to enrich the lives of others, and—if possible—to find a way to make a living doing it. I have worked hard over the years to do just that, and by God's grace, my life is joyful and full.

With his continued grace, it will continue to be joyful and full, because I will always seek to discover the gifts I have been given and look for more ways to use those gifts to enrich my life and the lives of others. For example, I have always loved writing, and over the years, I have prayed and learned to use that gift to write books that would lead others to have a deeper love of life, people, and God. I have also always loved music, and over the years I have prayed and worked to be good enough to share that gift in church, where every weekend I try to lead people into deeper worship of God. I have always been something of a ham, and over the years I have prayed and worked to learn how to use that gift to enrich the lives of others, which eventually led me to be the host of a daily radio show.

God deserves all the credit if I have accomplished anything. But he would not be able to use me at all unless I had ignored the advice of my relatives and instead of selling out my joy for insurance benefits, sought to pursue God's will for my life.

The secret to your fulfillment is discovering your gifts and constantly looking for new ways to use them to enrich the lives of others. Having listed your gifts above, take a few moments to reflect on some ways that you could use those gifts more fully to make others' lives easier, more pleasant, or more meaningful. Don't be afraid to be still. Just brainstorm. Write those ideas here.

1. _____

2. _____

3. _____

4. _____

If you were able to brainstorm some ideas, wait for a moment before you act, because I want to add one more qualifier that will increase the chances that whatever actions you take will result in a more joyful and fulfilling life. On the other hand, if you weren't able to come up with any ideas, be patient—you will have another chance in a minute. We have looked at the first two steps to pursuing joy: avoiding what is contrary to God's laws and discovering your gifts and using them for the good of others. Now we will take a look at the third step to finding fulfillment.

3. How can I pursue those gifts more fully in a manner that is respectful of the people he has placed in my life?

Knowing what your gifts are and having a desire to use those gifts to enrich the lives of others is important, but there is one more point to consider. You must not only use your gifts to work for the good of others; you must also do that in a manner that is good for the others in your life.

If you become so obsessed with pursuing your own interests that you are not sufficiently present to your spouse and children, for example, you will not be joyful. No matter how much you pour yourself into your interests and passions, no matter how much you work for the good of others in the world at large, if you are neglecting the primary "others" in your life, you will not be joyful. The most you can experience is pleasure when you do those things that interest you. As soon as you stop, however, you will be miserable, because you know that your spouse is upset and your children are suffering from your absence.

* * *

"I have to do what's best for me," said Paul. "My family just doesn't understand. I love what I do for a living and I want to be the best at it. I know it takes me away from them, but if they love me, they should understand. I don't get why they have to make things so difficult. My wife is constantly harping on me; my kids act like I'm public enemy number one. I have to use the gifts God gave me."

Paul is partially right. He does have to use the gifts he has been given, but when he uses them in an indiscriminate way, in a manner that threatens the primacy of his marriage and family relationships, then he is using those gifts imprudently. Joy never results from an imprudent use of gifts.

Compare Paul's experience to that of Lydia.

Lydia was a client of mine who felt unfulfilled in her life. She loved her role as a wife and stay-at-home mother of four, but she also felt that she was not using her gifts. She was an English and education major in college who loved teaching, but she felt that she could not put sufficient time into teaching and writing and still be the mother she wanted to be. Even so, she missed this very important part of her life.

"I feel like something is missing," Lydia said. "I love my kids and my life, but I always saw myself working in some capacity in English—teaching, writing, I don't know, something. I love the creative aspect of that work. I miss taking on new professional challenges. Of course, I always try to look for new ways to apply my creativity on the home front, and that really helps. Still, it would be fun if I could figure out a way to use what I'm good at more fully, as long as my children wouldn't have to suffer from my absence."

I challenged Lydia to brainstorm some ideas about how she could use her gifts—her love of English as well as her love for her family—in more creative and fulfilling ways. She got a funny smile on her face. At first, she resisted telling me what she was thinking, but finally she 'fessed up.

"Oh, I sometimes wonder about doing freelance editing work as well as doing some creative writing. I'm not sure how good I'd be at it, but I heard about an editor's test a large book publisher near us was giving, and I thought that if I did well on the test, perhaps I could begin to do some editing work from home, and that would give me some contacts in magazine publishing, too."

I thought the idea had merit. Here was a way she could use her unique gifts fully, and use them in a way that respected the relationships that were most important to her. I encouraged her to gather more information on the subject and to discuss the idea further with her husband. Over the next few weeks, she became more excited as she talked with publishing companies, signed up for a class on becoming a published writer, and eventually took the editing test, passing with outstanding marks.

Today, Lydia is thriving. She loves the challenge of helping other people focus their thoughts through her editing work, and she truly enjoys forming new ideas into her own stories. She has even found a way for her children to be involved in her work. She often makes up stories with them just for fun, and she recently asked her children to help her develop some ideas for a children's book she is currently proposing to an agent.

She feels more fulfilled than ever and looks forward to the future as well. She observed: "When I started using my gifts like this for the first time since I had kids—come to think of it, maybe the first time ever—I felt like I was able to bring all the different parts of me together. It's a good fit."

* * *

If you compare Paul's and Lydia's stories, you can get a sense of the difference between exercising gifts in a manner that is respectful of relationships and in a manner that is not. I don't, by the way, mean to imply that to utilize your gifts in a manner that is respectful of your primary relationships you must spend every waking hour with your family (though I'm sure you could do worse, and if you don't think so, perhaps you should look into that). But in order to lead to joy, your gifts must be exercised in a manner that is respectful of the people God has placed in your life.

I hope that in the course of this chapter I have at least started some wheels turning in your mind. Wherever you are in your life, God will get you to where he wants you to be if you prayerfully and doggedly follow the three simple steps I outline in this chapter. When considering how to pursue greater fulfillment in your life, rule out those options that oppose God's laws, make a sincere commitment to identifying and pursuing your gifts and using them for the good of others, and then exercise those gifts in a manner that is respectful of the primary relationships in your life.

In the next few chapters, we will examine the three most common obstacles you will encounter in attempting to take these steps: doubt, fear, and the sometimes strenuous objections of others.

FOUR

Act, Even When You Doubt

Randy had been coming to me to help clarify the next stage of his life. Dissatisfied with his career for a long time, the more he put himself through the process I described in the last chapter, the more he felt that God was leading him in the direction of opening an ice cream store. The problem was that he felt completely silly about his discernment.

"This is just stupid," he said in one session. "I know I've thought about opening an ice cream store from time to time over the years, but why would God want me to do this? Somehow I think that this is just my desire getting in the way of good discernment.

"I'm giving up a good job with great benefits to open an ice cream store? And I have the audacity to think that God is leading me to do it? I defy you, Greg, to try to convince me that I am not the biggest moron that ever walked the face of the earth."

* * *

I decided to start the chapter with this example because it seems so silly. Randy asked a valid question: Why *would* God

78

ask him to open an ice cream store? Was God really asking him to do such a thing? If so, why?

Or was Randy just out of his mind? Many people would say that he was. Randy certainly thought so.

Before I answer these questions, I want you to reflect on the path you are attempting to discern for your life. Does it seem silly, somehow not noble enough? Does it seem impossible, too difficult to get from where you are to where you think God might want you to be? How do you know whether God is *really* asking you to embrace this path? Is it merely the result of your own silly desires? These are some of the questions I want to address in the course of this chapter.

No Doubt about It

Doubt is the first obstacle we encounter when we try to act on what we think God might be leading us to do. How do we really know we are obeying God's will and not our own?

In the beginning, Adam and Eve had a perfect union with God. They could hear his voice clearly and know his will perfectly (even though, obviously, they didn't always follow it). After the Fall, though, the lines of communication all but collapsed for them and their descendants. Even now, after the life, death, and resurrection of the Lord Jesus, with all the grace that permeates all of humanity and time as a result, it can still be extremely difficult to know whether we are hearing God's voice and knowing his will correctly.

But let's get back to Randy for a minute. Why might God be calling him to do something seemingly as silly as opening an ice cream franchise?

Remember that in the first chapter, I said that God's path always leads in the direction of greater meaning, virtue, and intimacy. It just so happened in Randy's case that—professionally speaking, anyway—opening an ice cream store was the option most likely to cause him to grow in all three areas.

Even though he was making good money in his position as a management consultant, Randy had gotten to the place where he could do the work with his hands tied behind his back and blindfolded. He felt that he could remain comfortably in his position until his retirement in fifteen years, but he had achieved all that he had set out to do.

The more he thought about it, the more he realized that making this crazy move would force him to trust God in ways that he had never trusted him before. He would be making a radical shift in his life for no other reasons than these: First, it seemed viable and personally rewarding. And second, in prayer he felt that God might be leading him to do it.

Randy had always been a man with a plan. This would be the first time in his life when he wouldn't be completely sure where life was taking him. He felt that this situation would force him to look to God more completely than he ever had in his life.

Then Randy confessed something that he hadn't ever shared with me before. "The place that I would put the store," he noted, "is within walking distance of a college campus. Have you ever heard of the program called Theology on Tap?"

I told him that I had. Theology on Tap is a Catholic young adult outreach where Catholic laypeople, priests, and occasionally even bishops go to a local pub on a designated night of the week to talk about theology and answer questions about the faith.

"Well," continued Randy, "you know that because my dad was an alcoholic, I have a thing about people drinking. But I really like the Theology on Tap concept, and I was thinking that everybody likes ice cream. Maybe one night a week I could have a 'Sundae School' night. I would invite local pastors and professors to speak and answer questions about the faith.

"As an incentive, I could offer a dollar-a-scoop sundae bar with one free scoop to anyone who came to the talk. I thought that would be a good way to do something for the Lord for being so generous and leading me into this crazy thing. What do you think?"

Coming from anyone else, this idea might even come across as flighty and hopelessly pious. But knowing Randy as I did, I was fairly certain that if anyone could pull this off, he could do it. He had good business sense, a deep love for the Lord, and contacts all throughout the diocese and college as a result of his past work and charitable efforts.

As it happens, Randy did eventually decide to open his premium ice cream business in a location that was a stone's throw from the campus. And his Sundae School concept was a surprising success. Not only was it good for business (he scheduled it for Tuesdays, his slowest night), but people seemed to appreciate the casual atmosphere, the good ice cream, and the opportunity to ask questions about the faith from people who actually knew more than they did, but wouldn't talk down to them. Randy couldn't have been happier.

"A lot of people thought I was crazy when I told them I wanted to do this," he says. I know I wasn't so sure they ren't right. Looking back, though, I really see that this is what God wanted me to do—for now anyway.

"Who knows where my life will go next? I just want to serve him, and I am freer to do that now than I have ever been. I am more grateful and trusting of his will than I have ever been, too. This has been a good move for me."

Randy's story presents a wonderful opportunity to talk about how God can use even the simplest ideas to bring about both a growth in personal virtue as well as change on the wider scale.

Doubt: Part of the Process

In a sense, feelings of doubt are the growing pains that accompany the call to spiritual maturity. Doubt afflicted Abraham and Sarah, Jonah, Zacharias, even Peter and the apostles. I would suggest that even the Blessed Mother expressed at least some small measure of doubt when Gabriel told her that she was going to bear a child: "How can this be?" (Lk 1:34). Doubt has been a common bugaboo of even the most spiritually mature saints. In our own age, even Mother Theresa's diaries reveal that she struggled with periods of depression and doubt.

Doubt is a painfully common experience. It can occur anytime we are being asked by God to do something that seems beyond our ability, beyond our circumstances, or even beyond immediate reason. Yet all the holy men and women throughout history show us what the faithful response to doubt is. That response is best summarized by Mary's *fiat:* "Let it be [done] to me according to your word" (Lk 1:38).

Moving On

When God told Abraham and Sarah that their descendants would be as numerous as the stars, when God told Jonah to preach repentance to the Ninevites, when the angel told Zacharias that he would be father to a baby—and of all things, a baby named John—and when a teenage virgin was told that she would bear God's Son to the world, surely they struggled with doubts. Surely they were afraid. And yet, what made them holy men and women was that no matter how ridiculous the mission the Lord sent them seemed to be, or how incredible the promises he made to them appeared, they all said (though sometimes reluctantly—as in Jonah's case), "Lord, let it be done to me according to your Word."

Anyone who calls himself a Christian must do the same. We cannot hope to discover the purpose for which God put us on this planet unless we can faithfully follow his plan. But how do we know that it is his plan and not ours? How do we really know that we have added up all the facts correctly?

Checking Your Math

In the children's novel *The Silver Chair*, author C.S. Lewis relates the story of a little girl who is transported to the magical land of Narnia. When she arrives, she is thirsty. She desperately wants to take a drink from a stream, but she sees a lion named Aslan standing there beside the water.

Despite her attempts to get the lion to promise not to eat her if she turns her back on him to get a drink, Aslan refuses to reassure her. He tells her, in effect: Do what you need to do, trust me, and see what happens. In the story, Aslan portrays a kind of Christ figure; what the lion tells the little girl, Christ may sometimes tell us.

Sometimes, God will give us "signs." He will submit to our simple, foolish tests to prove his will to us. The biblical character Gideon had his fleece, and we have our modern-day versions as well: flipping through random Bible passages, looking for significant coincidences, and so on.

Nevertheless, as much as I have been tempted and continue to be tempted to use these means of "discernment" to gain reassurance from God that I am on the right path, I find that God does not always like to be tested. He prefers that we use the gifts he has already given us—our intellect, the stirrings of our heart, and our developing relationship with him—to discern the course he would like us to take without his having to lead us by the nose every step of the way.

Too often, we are like the little girl in the Narnia story. We see the water in front of us and we long to take a drink. But we are afraid that trouble will swallow us whole if we stop looking at it. We want to step out in faith, but we want to be "sure" first.

Yet if we are sure, then is it really stepping out in faith? I would argue that it is not. God often draws the plans he has for our lives with dotted lines and then gives us the gift of faith to fill in the spaces.

Unfortunately, too many people don't want faith; they want proof. Though they are certainly well-meaning, inevitably these individuals die of thirst as they stand right next to the water because they are afraid to act without proof that trouble will not devour them. They say, "I would take these steps that I believe to be God's plan for healing my relationship, my career, or my life, but I cannot act until God demonstrates to me beyond all reasonable doubt that it will work."

When they do this, they forget that faith is not proof. It is trust.

If we have prayerfully gone through the steps I described in the last chapter, regardless of where those steps have led us, we must assume that the path we are walking is true.

Dealing with a Difficult Marriage: Brenda's Story

Brenda was miserable in her marriage. Her husband, Philip, was verbally abusive and cruel. He regularly insulted her, dismissed her concerns, and terrorized her and their children with his temper.

By using the methods I described in the last chapter, she came to believe that the correct thing to do was to tell her husband that she loved him, but things had to change. Unless he promised to enroll in an anger management class at the local mental health center, and undergo an evaluation for the depression that we believed was the source of his anger, he would have to leave until he did. She did not wish to divorce him, and had no intention of doing so, but she could not continue to live with him, or subject her children to him if he persisted in acting as he did.

Brenda had prayed consistently about this course of action. That prayer, combined with the fact that many, many, many other gentler means to reach out to her husband had failed, narrowed our realistic, healthy, godly options to the plan I just described. Still, she was so terrified that she couldn't act on the plan.

"How do I know this is right? It just doesn't feel right. I feel afraid. Shouldn't I feel peaceful if this is really the right way to go? If I blow this, there is so much at stake. What if I'm wrong? What if I'm just running away?"

All of her objections made sense on a certain level, but having ruled out all other possible healthy options, this was the only choice left. When we would talk, and when she would pray, she would be a bit calmer, even though the anxiety and the doubts never went away completely. In these moments, her mind would be a little quieter, and she knew that this was the right thing to do. Still, as soon as she would walk away from these quieter times of reflection, the doubts and anxiety would come surging back, and she would feel paralyzed.

Finally, six months later, Brenda found the courage to go to her husband and outline the plan we had been discussing. He was furious at first, but she managed to hold her ground. She kept repeating that she loved him and that she hoped he would choose well, but he had to decide whether he would take active steps to learn to control his anger, or move out until he did.

He threatened, he cajoled, and in an ironic but not unexpected turn of events, he even accused her of trying to control and manipulate him. But she stood firm.

Brenda had never been able to stand up to him like that before. Even though she told me she was shaking so hard that she felt as if everything on the inside was going to fall outside, she kept doing what she had discerned was right. The pressure and tension with her husband kept up for about two weeks, but each time he tried to argue with her, she refused to fight with him and simply repeated her statement calmly and charitably. She hoped that he would choose her and his children, but he couldn't hold onto both them and his abusive manner. He would have to choose them or go.

The day came when she was within two days of packing up his things, moving them to a hotel, and calling him at work to tell him not to come home until he had gotten help. At dinner that evening, however, he told her he had made an appointment for the following week with the anger management counselor. She couldn't believe it.

"This last couple of weeks were awful," she said, "but not much more awful than usual, and at least this time I had a cause worth fighting for. If I had known this would really work, I would have done it months ago. I can't believe how much time I wasted doubting myself and my discernment. I didn't just put up with this for months; I've been living like this for years."

Brenda and her husband still had a long way to go, but through the process I described in the last chapter, God led her to the next step. In fact, he had been leading her to this step for years, but she had been too doubtful and afraid to act on what she inherently knew had been the right thing from the start.

Brenda's circumstances provide a good example of what must happen. Your situation might be completely different. Perhaps your struggle is not in your marriage, but in dealing with a prodigal child or confronting a disheartening work life. Whatever the situation, if you feel frustrated and disappointed, and if you are anything like the rest of us, I can promise you there are a million and one ways you are getting in your own way with doubt and anxiety.

Job Loss: Harry's Story

Harry provides another example. With only a high school diploma, Harry got in on the ground floor of an engineering business. Over the course of twenty years, he worked his way up in the company to a position where most of his colleagues had at least master's degrees in engineering. He distinguished himself among his peers, and the few that found out about his educational background were amazed at what he was capable of.

Then the company changed hands. Harry was passed over for several plum projects that he would have been the first choice for under the previous ownership. When he finally began complaining after several months of this treatment, he was called into a meeting with members of upper management.

Harry felt confident at the time that he would be able to work things out in this meeting. He was just pleased that they were willing to listen. But when he arrived in the conference room that day, he found that his employers were ready to do anything but listen.

After thanking him for all his years of service to the company, they informed Harry that the company would be "moving in a new direction," and they did not see him as part of that direction. The management listened politely while Harry tried to defend himself, but after a few minutes, they suggested that he continue this conversation with the human resources person who was present because the rest of the attendees had another meeting to attend. Before Harry knew it, he was in the middle of his exit interview.

The HR representative explained that in light of his years of dedication, he would be given a three-month severance. Also, in order to give him time to "begin investigating new options," as the HR representative put it, Harry was told that he would have until the end of the day to clean out his office, and that there would be no need to return after that.

Things were difficult for Harry. He was unab
another job in his field. Prospective employers all took one
look at his educational background and gave him a polite pass.

He began seriously looking at want ads for the menial jobs
that would accept his high school degree. He thought about
going to college, but he needed to make a living now, and at
forty-seven, he didn't think that he would be any more
employable with a college degree at age fifty-one than he was
without one now.

I told Harry that I certainly understood how pressured he
must feel. But since he had a little time left before he had to
begin working somewhere—anywhere—I led him through
the process I described in the last chapter. I especially had him
consider other gifts and talents God had given him and how
he could use those skills to lead a more abundant life.

The only thing he could come up with was that he
enjoyed woodworking. He seemed to have a natural gift for it,
but his father, a carpenter, had discouraged him from the
trades when he was a boy because he wanted his son to have
an easier life. Even so, Harry had spent many hours over the
years in furniture making and woodcarving. In fact, he had
built much of the furniture in his home, including the four-
poster Shaker-style bed he made for his wife one Christmas.

Harry had always harbored a secret wish to be able to
make a living at what had merely been his expensive hobby.
He wanted to be a fine furniture maker. After much prayer
and discernment on his part, and many conversations between
us, Harry decided to do three things.

First, he would take a class in master woodworking, both
to polish his skills and to see how capable he really was.
Second, he would make a portfolio of photographs of the
pieces he had done that he felt had the most potential for sales.

Finally, he would present his work to a few select furniture stores in his area and take part in a local artisans' festival with the intention of gaining some commissions from individuals.

Harry took the first two steps with ease. But when it came down to actually making presentations to the stores and contacting the representatives of the artisans' festival, the doubts came rushing forward.

"I've always just done this for fun. I don't know if I really have what it takes to do this on a professional basis. Besides, I don't know anything about running my own business. I have always worked for somebody else. Do I really want the headaches of handling angry clients, carrying overhead and inventory, and selling myself and my work?"

By now, Harry and I had a solid counseling relationship, so I felt I could be a little more direct with him than I usually might. I asked Harry—somewhat tongue-in-cheek—whether he had begun rethinking his rewarding career in the ever-expanding field of grocery bagging. He took my point.

Harry had a choice to make. He could confront this serious challenge he was living through with eyes of faith—which could lead him to take the risks necessary for living a more abundant life. Or he could allow this experience to diminish him, to rob him of his dignity and passion for the sake of "security" or the easy path.

Harry and I had talked enough by now for him to know that God never asks us to move backward, only further ahead, constantly expanding our skills, our practice of virtue, and our trust in his divine providence. The doubt he experienced was a natural part of growth, but it did not come from God. If the doubt about starting this woodworking business had been leading him to consider an even more rewarding, more challenging, but equally viable alternative, then I would have said that we would need to give more serious consideration to it. However, this doubt would only lead him in an undesirable direction, a direction that he felt diminished by—so clearly this doubt did not point down any path that led to an abundant life.

If he failed at this business, there would always be time to pursue safer options. Nevertheless, I argued, he owed it to God to take this opportunity to use to the fullest the gifts the Lord had given him.

Finally, I asked him to imagine what life might be like five years from now if he were successful. I asked him to imagine that getting off the ground had been a rather stop-and-go process, but that in subsequent years, the orders had become more frequent and that his work had become more widely known. I then asked him to consider what it would be like doing something he loved and making an even better living than he had been making before in a job he simply liked well enough.

I looked him in the eyes and asked him: If you were standing five years in the future, looking back on the present difficulty from this position of relative success, would it have been worth all the pain and struggle of losing your job in order to get to this place?

He agreed that it would. With that, I told him that from a faith perspective, as well as from a counseling perspective, I didn't see that he had any other choice but to try to move forward.

He had used the gifts God had given him—his intellect, will, and talents—to devise a plan. He had prayed for wisdom before developing the plan. He had prayed for guidance while devising it, and he had continued to pray for God's blessing and confirmation of the plan now that it was outlined.

What more could he do? There were only two things left to do: First, he could act on the plan. Second, he could continue praying: If somehow Harry had added up all the facts wrong, he could ask God in his mercy to point him in the right direction gently but obviously. And if Harry had indeed discerned God's will correctly, he could pray that God would bless his plan and give him the courage to follow it through.

Harry agreed with this analysis. Shortly after our conversation, we ended our sessions. I didn't see him for several years, but when I later needed a set of wall-to-wall bookshelves built, I happened to think of him. I called the only phone number I had for him to see how he was and whether he wanted the work.

Harry told me that he was glad to hear from me after all this time and that he would be happy to take my order. But he would have to put me on a six-month waiting list! He apologized for having to ask me to wait, but he explained that he was swamped with orders both from stores and individual clients—so much so that he had hired two assistant craftsmen to help him. I told him how pleased I was to hear the pleasure—and the exhaustion—in his voice, and that it would be my honor to wait as long as he needed me to wait, just as long as I knew that he would personally build my bookcases.

Walk Toward the Door

Harry's story illustrates an important part of battling doubt—the determination to pursue a more meaningful, more abundant life, no matter how frightening that may seem.

Once you have taken the steps I outlined in the last chapter to get a basic idea of what God's plan for the next step in your life might be, you will confront doubts: Did I get it right? What if this isn't God's will, but only mine?

The only answer I have for you is this: If you have taken the steps in a spirit of prayer and you have been sincerely seeking God's wisdom throughout the process, then you have no other choice but to assume that you have gotten it right unless God makes it absolutely, unmistakably obvious that he wants you to do something else.

Of course, the doubter will ask, "How will I know if he wants me to do something else?" I believe that the answer to this question will be clear if you are thinking in terms of pursuing a more abundant life. If, as you are walking down the path you have discerned, God suddenly shows you an unmistakably more viable opportunity for achieving even greater meaning, intimacy, and virtue, then take it. Short of that, you must pursue the path you have discerned. Period.

If you talk to those who consider their lives to be fulfilling—whether or not they meet anyone else's definition of success—they will tell you that it was not easy to get to where they are. Nor will it be easy to continue to travel their path. But they do continue walking down that path because, in their eyes, there are no other viable options available.

Objectively, of course, this simply may not be true. For example, you might look at someone's life and say, "How odd that you pursued this path as opposed to just living in your mother's basement, or going to work in this unfulfilling, unrewarding, but seemingly safer job. How strange that you chose not to settle for this person as a spouse when it looked as if there were no other choices."

No doubt, looking from the outside in, you could very well pick out at least a hundred more paths such a life could have taken. No doubt such individuals were not unaware of those options, but they made a conscious decision to pursue abundance (that is, meaning, virtue, and intimacy) at the cost of the illusion of security and even their immediate comfort. They consciously ruled out other options as unthinkable, because those options did not lead to abundance. And when they ran their choices through this sieve, all they were left with was the path they were taking.

This is the same perspective you must have if you are serious about fulfilling the purpose for which you were created. Having discerned a path, you must continue to walk down it, toward abundance, no matter how dark the valleys seem between where you are and where abundance waits.

In discussing this matter with my clients, I often use the image of being in a dark room with many doors. The room is so dark that some of the doors are hard to see. Each door has a sign on it that hints at what lies behind it, but it makes no promises. It is just a door.

Our job is to discern, based upon what we can see, which door is most likely to lead toward abundance. But because we can't see every door in this dark room, we often wonder whether we are missing something, and this sense manifests itself as doubt. We must be respectful of the doubt we feel, because it allows us to step cautiously and forces us to be attentive to other possibilities.

Yet even so, we cannot allow ourselves to be paralyzed by such doubt. Having made a decision to walk toward a particular door, we must take a step. Then we must stop, pray, and look around again.

Ask yourself: From this new position, having prayed and asked for the light of grace to shine, do I see another door that would obviously lead to an even more abundant life than the door I am walking toward? If the answer is yes, then by all means you should walk toward that new door. On the other hand, if you cannot see any new doors, or the doors you see, though new, do not seem to lead to a more abundant life than the door you are currently walking toward, then keep walking toward the door you discerned to be the correct one in the first place! That door remains your best option.

Take another step and repeat the process—and so on, and on, until you have either been led, step-by-step, in a completely new direction, or you are standing in front of the door you originally discerned to be the correct one. If you use this *step, pray, discern, repeat* process, you can assume that you are in God's will and that he will lead you properly. Keep walking forward despite the doubt you feel.

Remember, Scripture tells us that "faith is . . . the conviction of things not seen" (Heb 11:1). Let faith and trust fill in the gaps between what you believe you are capable of and what God knows you are capable of. Praying through this process one step at a time will allow you to have a healthy respect for the gift of doubt without allowing yourself to become paralyzed by it.

Now that we have taken a look at strategies for addressing doubt, the next chapter will confront the next obstacle to overcoming disappointment and frustration in your life: the anxiety you face as you begin actually walking through the door you're now standing before.

FIVE

Investigate the Causes of Your Anxiety

After doubt, the next obstacle we encounter is *anxiety*. Doubt and anxiety are related, of course, but for our purposes, I will make some important distinctions.

On the one hand, doubt is the first enemy we face when we are discerning God's will. Doubt makes it difficult to be sure about the direction in which our discernment is pointing us. It forces us to stand paralyzed, never allowing us to get out of the gate, leaving us dithering about what first steps we should take.

By comparison, anxiety is what we experience when we are a little farther down the road. It is what happens once we have decided that we know what God wants us to do, but we just aren't capable of it. It is the feeling Noah had when he knew God wanted him to build an ark, and all his neighbors started laughing at him. It is what Jonah felt once he was convinced that God really was serious about that whole "Go to Nineveh" thing.

While doubt causes us to ask, Am I doing the right thing? Anxiety causes us to ask, Am I up to the challenge? Do I have what it takes to meet the challenges successfully that I will face on the other side of this door I have chosen? In this chapter, it is my hope to prove that you are capable of much more than you think. God already knows this; it's time you did, too.

* * *

Mark, age forty-four, needs to make a change.

"I know I need to get out of this job," he says. "It's sucking up all my time and energy. I don't have anything left for my family anymore, much less myself, but I don't know where else I would go or how I would get there. I have obligations. I think I could probably make it somewhere else, but I get afraid. What if I fail? What if it doesn't work out? Then what?"

* * *

Ginny, age thirty-seven, knows that her marriage needs serious help, but she is terrified of making an issue out of it. She puts it this way:

"Fred just isn't the kind of person who will go to therapy or even a Marriage Encounter or Retrouvaille Weekend. He hates having to open up to people, and he takes even the slightest criticism personally. That's what stops me from ever really addressing our problems.

"I get ready to bring these things up, and then I get terrified. I start thinking, *What if he gets fed up with me? What if he thinks that all I ever do is complain and he says he wants to leave me? What would I do then? How would I handle it?* Then I start thinking that maybe it's just better I keep quiet."

* * *

Sometimes, even when we think we know that God wants us to make a change in our lives, that isn't enough. We tell ourselves that the devil we know is better than the devil we don't, and that excuses us from ever having to take action to become the people that God is calling us to be and to have the relationships he is calling us to have. In the end, our fear gets the better of us, and our lives pay the price as they become smaller and smaller.

In my book, *God Help Me! This Stress Is Driving Me Crazy!* (Crossroad, 2010), I examine the many ways anxiety tries to stop us from fulfilling God's plan for our lives. Anxiety seems ever present, but for the Christian, life is about leaving behind our anxieties and placing more and more trust in the Lord. Psychologist and spiritual director Fr. Benedict Groeschel observes in his book *Spiritual Passages* (Crossroad, 1984) that Christians progress through the three stages of spiritual maturity: the *purgative* way, in which we turn away from the most obvious sin in our lives; the *illuminative* way, in which we begin to manifest the first signs of spiritual maturity and gain greater wisdom and spiritual insight; and the *unitive* way, in which we achieve an almost nuptial union with God. In this process, he notes, the experience of anxiety decreases as trust in God's providence increases.

Leaving behind anxiety is such an important part of the Christian walk that the Catholic Church places a prayer known as the *Embolism* smack-dab in the middle of the Our Father: "Deliver us, Lord, from every evil *and protect us from all anxiety . . .*" (emphasis mine). Even Scripture tells us, "Have no anxiety about anything" (Phil 4:6).

Why is it so important to leave behind our anxieties? Because anxiety causes a kind of spiritual suffocation that is the antithesis of the peace beyond all understanding that Jesus came to give those who love him and follow in his ways (see Phil 4:7).

The Lord said, "I came that they may have life, and have it abundantly" (Jn 10:10). Of course, he was talking about the fulfillment that comes from eternal life, but I contend that he also came that we might know the fullness of this life as well. Yet if we are so choked by anxiety that we cannot proclaim his truth, or stand up for what is just, or if we allow our anxiety to make us so self-protective that we cannot exhibit Christian charity, then how can we be living the abundant life Christ calls us to?

Granted, there is such a thing as prudence, and sometimes, fear is a function of prudence. I feel afraid, with good reason, to walk through a crime-ridden neighborhood alone at midnight. It is not prudent to do so. But while prudence is the fear that causes me to avoid the things that would be dangerous to my physical, moral, or emotional health, anxiety is the fear that causes me to avoid the very things that I have determined would be good for me.

At the beginning of this chapter, I gave the example of two people who were paralyzed by anxiety. Both had used the techniques I described in the last chapter to discern prayerfully that God was calling them to make a change in their lives. But both were paralyzed by the fear they encountered when it came down to making that change. That is what anxiety does: It stops us from following through on the actions we have discerned to be essential to our physical, emotional, and moral health.

Over the next few pages, we will take a look at anxiety, where it comes from, and how to overcome it.

Where Does Anxiety Come From?

All emotions find their origin in something psychologists call *automatic thoughts*. These thoughts represent the meanings we assign to events that occur, meanings that tell us how we should feel about a situation.

Let's say you ask me to help you with something, but I, regrettably, tell you that I cannot help you because I have a previous commitment that I cannot break. Your *interpretation* of that refusal—the automatic thought that you have in response to that refusal—will ultimately determine how you feel about it.

For example, perhaps the automatic thought that runs through your mind is "Greg is usually a pretty generous guy; if he could help me, he would." You would feel disappointed at my refusal of your request, but you would also be sympathetic to my position.

But what if the automatic thought was different? What if what went through your head was "What a jerk! Doesn't he know how important this is to me? He is so selfish." In that case, you would be furious with me, even if all the facts of the situation were exactly the same.

Let's take another automatic thought that could result from the same situation: "I have to do *everything* by myself. Nobody cares about me. Life isn't fair!" Now, in addition to feeling disappointed, you will feel depressed.

We could sit around for the next month coming up with different permutations of this situation. Each slightly different interpretation would lead to a different emotional experience. The funny thing is that the facts of the situation won't have changed one bit. You asked for help, and while I was sympathetic, I had a very good reason for refusing. Period. But the interpretation makes it a very different experience for you according to your automatic thought.

The same is true for anxiety. Automatic thoughts are the source of every anxious feeling that stops us from doing those things that, in our more lucid moments, we discern would be in our best interests.

* * *

Cheryl would like to be more involved in her community. She often thinks that she would like to run for the local school board. She has a gift for organization and a heart for children.

When she prays about it, she has a good feeling about the idea, her husband supports her, and they even know that it would not infringe on their family commitments in any unmanageable way. All signs seem to point to *"Go."* But as the time approaches to register for the election, she decides to pass.

"Who do I think I am, anyway?" she asks. "All the other people running are professionals. I have never worked outside the home. What do I have to offer? They would laugh me off the street."

* * *

Gillian is a nurse in the oncology unit. She enjoys her work, but sometimes the stress of her particular work environment is too much, and the schedule isn't the best as far as she is concerned. Recently, she had the opportunity to work in a new chemotherapy clinic that was opening. It looked like a great opportunity.

The position required some administrative responsibilities, something she had wanted to have for some time. The pay was better, and the schedule was straight 7-3 with no shift work. Ideal for her. When she prayed about the situation, she had a good feeling about the change, and there was certainly nothing to stop her from taking the position from a moral perspective.

In the end, though, she declined.

"I know I'm probably going to regret it," she admitted. "But I just don't feel up to it. I get nervous in new situations. I'm not really all that happy where I am, but I don't know . . . maybe it's just better that I stay put."

* * *

Robert had the opportunity to move his florist shop to a new location. The building he was in stood in an older part of town, and he was not generating the kind of traffic he thought he might if he moved. The problem was that the rent was higher in the new location.

He thought he could handle it, but what if business dropped off? He tried to run some numbers, and on paper it looked really good. He kept taking it to God in prayer and it seemed right. Still, what if?

"I would hate to risk everything I've built here," he said. "What if it doesn't work out? I'm not happy with the way things are going, but that's still better than declaring bankruptcy." In the end, despite strong feelings and evidence to the contrary, he decided to stay put. "Better safe than sorry, I guess."

Unfortunately, as time went by, the neighborhood deteriorated further. His traffic continued to decrease until he was trapped. He could neither afford to move nor afford to stay open where he was. He was forced to file for bankruptcy and close his store.

* * *

Each of these examples illustrates the false thoughts that lie at the root of anxiety. Cheryl's automatic thoughts stopped her from using her gifts in a fulfilling way, even though she had both a desire to serve and the support of her family. Gillian was unable to take a job that would have been ideal for her because her automatic thoughts told her that she should listen to her anxiety even though it was completely unfounded. And Robert's automatic thoughts eventually led him to financial ruin, ironically, by telling him that taking an appropriate risk was too risky.

In each case, we see perfectly normal people making "safe" choices, not because they are truly safe, but because they are too anxious to do what is truly good for them. I believe that Satan loves this situation. Each time we make a "safe" choice—not a choice that is truly prudent, mind you, but a choice that mostly results from trying to avoid our anxiety—we act like the man in Jesus' famous parable of the talents who buried his gifts in a hole because he was afraid of losing them.

The result is that our life gets smaller and smaller until we become crushed by it. The disappointments of life mount up, largely because of our own lack of fortitude, and we feel confused, saying, "I did the best I could"—when, in fact, we didn't. We failed to heed our Lord's warning. All along the path, we loved our lives, our comfort, our security, just a little too much, and we lost it, bit by bit.

There is a saying that the battle for the soul is waged in the mind. I believe that this is absolutely true. Every day, people call me and say, "Greg, I pray and I pray, and nothing ever changes. Why has God abandoned me?"

The fact is, when we pray, God does answer. He pours out his grace and lights the path he is calling us to follow out of the darkness in which we find ourselves. But because our minds are so clouded by false, anxiety-producing thoughts, we are unable to see that light.

We look around, but we can't see a way out. The false, automatic thoughts serve as blinders that cause us to see only the few unattractive options in front of us. Meanwhile, we don't notice the airplane-hangar-sized door God is opening *behind* us.

Routing out the false thoughts that cause anxiety is key to being able to fulfill the purpose for which we were created. The acronym TRUTH represents the five steps to overcoming false thoughts and discovering the path God would have us walk:

Trust the mission God places on your heart.
Recognize your automatic thoughts.
Use the "abundant life test" (see pg 108) to separate true thoughts from false thoughts.
Testify to what is true.
Have courage and step out in faith.

Throughout the rest of this chapter, we will examine what it means to live in the TRUTH, one step at a time.

Trust the Mission God Places on Your Heart

We examined this step rather thoroughly in the last chapter, but the point of mentioning it here is that it is not enough to discern the ultimate goal toward which God wants you to work. It takes commitment to reach that goal. Many people think that if God wants them to do something, it will come easily. This is not usually the case.

Remember, in God's eyes, more important than our achieving the goal is our pursuing the meaning, intimacy, and virtue that will ultimately result in our joy. But meaning, intimacy, and virtue are all hard-won qualities. They do not come by my rolling out of bed in the morning and falling into the plan God has already fulfilled for me in my sleep. They come from my picking up my cross every day, and striving, as St. Paul says, to work out my own salvation "with fear and trembling" (Phil 2:12).

Scripture tells us that we will be tested in the fires of affliction as we pursue the mission God has created us to fulfill (see 1 Pt 4:12). This is where many of us go wrong. We may be confident in the gifts God has given us. We may have some ideas about how to use those gifts for the good of others. We may even have figured out a course of action that will allow us to pursue that call in a manner that is respectful of the others in our life.

Nevertheless, having done all that, we expect that God will place our goal in a neat little gift-wrapped package and hand it to us with a pretty bow tied on top. But where is the virtue in that?

You must have confidence in the mission God has given you even when the struggle comes. Do your best to pray and discern what God wants you to do with your gifts. Then, while you continue to pray, keep moving ahead no matter how difficult it may seem.

Ask God to give you the virtue of fortitude. On those hard days when you doubt whether or not you have discerned the Lord's will correctly, you should, of course, take the question back to prayer. But unless you receive a dramatic response that unquestionably changes your mind, you must press on through the fear and doubt. You must trust that, since you are constantly seeking his will and testing that will to the best of your ability, God will find a way to get through your thick skull what his real will is, or his silence means you are indeed on the right track.

Recognize Your Automatic Thoughts

Automatic thoughts, as we saw earlier, are the thoughts that cause our emotional reactions. In order to understand whether the anxiety we are feeling is a prudent reaction to a foolish action we are attempting to undertake, or a temptation to forsake the path down which God has commanded us to walk, we need to know what thoughts are actually guiding our emotions.

As you imagine pursuing the path you think God might want you to travel, how do you feel? Do you feel confident? Anxious? Confused?

Well, how do you know whether that confidence is false? How do you know whether the anxiety is justified? How do you know whether you are really confused or simply don't want to admit to yourself what you know to be true? The only way to tell is by first recognizing, and then analyzing, the automatic thoughts that are causing whatever emotional reaction you are experiencing.

Many people make the process of recognizing automatic thoughts much more complicated than it needs to be. Here's what you do.

Step One: Write down the situation.

Write one sentence describing the situation that is causing your anxiety. For example: "I have to tell my husband that we need to get some counseling." Or "I need to give notice to my employer." Keep the statement short. Leave out any analysis; that will come later. Just state the simple fact.

Step Two: Attempt to justify your emotional reaction.

Now that you have written down the anxiety-producing situation, it's time to get to the automatic thoughts. Ask yourself the following questions: What does this situation mean to me? Why do I feel justified in being anxious or upset? Or you might ask yourself: If I had to justify this emotional reaction to someone, what would I say?

Write four or five sentences in answer to the questions above. These sentences represent the automatic thoughts that are going through your mind as you contemplate doing what you prayerfully believe is God's will for your life. Combining steps one and two, the result might look something like these examples.

Situation:

I have to tell my husband that we need to get some counseling.

Automatic thoughts:

I'm afraid. What if he gets angry? What if he tells me I'm silly for wanting to go for marriage counseling? Then I will feel even worse than I do already. Maybe I should just keep quiet.

Situation:

I have to give notice to my employer.

Automatic thoughts:

This is crazy! Why would I give up a good job just to pursue some pipe dream? Why should I play games with my security? What if my idea doesn't work? Then where will I be?

  In both of these situations, you see the kinds of thoughts that are going through these individuals' heads. Is it any wonder that they are doubting whether or not God is calling them to do what they think he might be calling them to do?

  Now that we've identified the automatic thoughts that lie behind the anxious and doubting emotions, it's time to see whether those thoughts are true or false, godly or ungodly. For that we go to the next letter in our acronym.

Use the "Abundant Life Test" to Separate True Thoughts From False Thoughts

If an automatic thought is true and godly, it ought to be followed. But how do we know whether our thoughts are true? Use the "abundant life test."

Jesus said, "I came that they may have life, and have it abundantly" (Jn 10:10). He did not say, "I came that you might be suffocated by the walls of your life closing in on you, just so long as you learn to offer it up." Yet so many of us live exactly that sort of life.

Why? Because, truth be told, even though it would be infinitely more rewarding, we do not really want to live the life God has for us; we want to live a life that we can manage on our own resources. We are afraid to believe that God really does love us enough to want us to live abundantly.

Nevertheless, he does. He says so, over and over in Scripture. "If you then, who are evil, know how to give good gifts to your children, how much more will your Father who is in heaven give good things to those who ask him!" (Mt 7:11). Now, it's important to remember: I am not saying that God cares much about your happiness (that is, your creature comforts, entertainment, and personal wealth). Rather, I am saying that God does desire that you pursue greater meaning, intimacy, and virtue in your life, and in return, you will receive the joy that comes from those pursuits.

The fact of the matter is that there is infinitely more joy to be found in pursuing an abundant life than in settling for a mediocre one. Where is the virtue in mediocrity?

Did Jesus really die so that I could ignore what he wanted me to do and instead cling to my 401 (k) and health insurance? Or so that I would be so nervous about getting the help I need to have an intimate, meaningful, virtuous marriage and family life that I would be willing to settle for a distant, shallow, and ignoble one? Somehow, I doubt it.

Now that you've identified the automatic thoughts that are causing the anxiety you feel about doing what you believe God has led you to, I want you to go through those thoughts, one sentence at a time, and ask yourself: Does this thought lead me in some way to pursue a more abundant life—that is, a life of greater meaningfulness, intimacy, and virtue?

If it does, then you may assume that the thought is true and godly and should be accepted. On the other hand, if it does not, you must assume that the thought is really Satan's attempt to talk you out of doing God's will. God's ways lead to an abundance of meaning, intimacy, and virtue. Satan's path leads to confusion, suffocation, estrangement, and sin. Which path are your thoughts leading you down?

Let's go back to our examples for a moment.

Situation:

I have to tell my husband that we need to get some counseling.

Automatic thoughts:

I'm afraid. What if he gets angry? What if he tells me I'm silly for wanting to do marriage counseling? Then I will feel even worse than I do already. Maybe I should just keep quiet.

Situation:

I have to give notice to my employer.

Automatic thoughts:

This is crazy! Why would I give up a good job just to pursue some pipe dream? Why should I play games with my security? What if my idea doesn't work? Then where will I be?

As you read through those automatic thoughts, you might be tempted to think many things. You might think, *Wow, these two people are dealing with some very challenging circumstances.* You might think, *They really have some hard decisions to make.* You might even think, *I sure am glad I'm not them.* (This last thought would be wrong, of course, because the anxiety we experience in the face of doing God's will makes you and me exactly like them, though details of our circumstances may differ.)

The one thing you could not think, however, is this: *Those thoughts they wrote down sure do lead to a more abundant life!* No. Those thoughts may lead to a seemingly safer life, a questionably more secure life, a possibly less conflicted life, but they will not, under any circumstances, lead to a more abundant life. Therefore they are false. They represent Satan's attempt to distract these poor people from the difficult though ultimately rewarding path God would have them travel.

If the two people in our examples choose to do what these thoughts are telling them, they are allowing themselves to become unwitting pawns in Satan's plan of destruction for their lives and relationships. No matter how much they pray for grace or deliverance, if they choose to act on these thoughts, they will be unable to see God's light and hear his voice. They will have allowed Satan to close their eyes and plug their ears.

I am often surprised by the number of people who tell me that they cannot hear God's voice in their hearts or clearly discern his will. I am surprised because I have been hearing it all my life, and frankly, if God sees fit to speak to the likes of me, then he can't wait to talk to you. God does not like me better than anyone else. If he is talking to me, then he wants to talk to you as well.

The only difference between us, perhaps, is that by being led by my parents into a deep personal encounter with the Lord from an early age, God showed me early on how to distinguish his voice from the noise Satan tries to play in my ear. He has also led me to discover the psychological techniques that confirm and perfect what he had already taught me on a gut level was true.

But you, too, can learn these things. By submitting your thoughts to the "abundant life test," you will learn to hear God speaking to your heart. So let's take a look at the next step.

Testify to What Is True

Once you've identified whether your automatic thoughts are pointing you in the direction of a more abundant life, and assuming that they are not (they so rarely do), you have to testify to what is true. You have to speak the truth to yourself.

Let me show you what I mean.

In our first example, a woman is afraid to tell her husband about her dissatisfaction with their marriage and her desire to seek counseling. Her automatic thoughts tell her to remain quiet and ignore the Holy Spirit's stirring in her heart, pushing her toward greater intimacy, meaning, and virtue in her relationship. Having identified those thoughts for what they are, false thoughts that lead to a smaller, less meaningful, estranged life, she has decided that even though the feelings are compelling and the thoughts persuasive, she must talk herself through them. Here is what she wrote.

True Thoughts:

Even though I am afraid, I've prayed about this and I know that there is no way our marriage can become more meaningful, intimate, or virtuous unless we get some outside help. I can't do what I feel. I must do what I have prayerfully discerned is right.

I must trust that God will protect me and give me the courage I need to do his will in my marriage. I must pray that he will give me the strength to speak the truth, to stand up for what I think is just, and to do both of those things as charitably as possible. I will continue to pray that I will stay in his will and that God's Spirit will guide me when I feel afraid or confused.

Compare these thoughts to the previous, false automatic thoughts, and you can see how much more likely it is that these thoughts would lead to more virtue, meaning, and intimacy, and therefore, to a more joyful, abundant life.

Now let's look at our second example, In it, a man faces having to give notice to his employer in order to pursue an opportunity that he has prayerfully discerned could be better and more fulfilling.

His automatic thoughts are telling him that he is being foolish risking his present security to pursue the unknown, even though he has tested and prayed about it and seen that it seems viable. His thoughts are telling him to ignore his intellect and discernment and stay put because he might fail. Here is what he wrote to challenge his false thoughts.

True Thoughts:

The decision to leave my present, secure position is nerve-wracking. But I have done my best to investigate all the possible problems, and all the evidence seems to suggest that this is the best path to take despite the fear I feel. I will continue to try to address any remaining concerns fully so that I can make sure that my fear is not trying to point out problems that I am missing.

Nevertheless, in the end I must do what I prayerfully and intellectually believe is best, regardless of what my feelings are telling me. I must pray for the wisdom to know God's will, and the courage to follow it no matter where it leads and no matter how many obstacles appear in my path. I will also pray that if I am discerning this incorrectly, God will be merciful and lead me back to the right path.

Even so, unless he makes it abundantly obvious that he does not want me to continue down this road, I have to assume that this is the way he wants me to go. I have to be faithful to what I believe is his will for my life. I know that if I can pull this off, my situation really would be better; I'm just afraid.

Nevertheless, fear—in the absence of any hard evidence—isn't a good enough reason to avoid what I believe God is leading me to do.

Clearly, there is much more virtue and meaning in this response, as well as a more intimate connection to God, than in the automatic thoughts we recorded above. Having realized that the automatic thoughts he was experiencing were actually leading him away from a more abundant life, the man in this example forced himself to reckon with what was really true, as opposed to what he merely felt was true.

I would like to add one qualifying note about this part of the exercise: I hope it is obvious from the examples I gave that testifying to the truth is different from giving yourself an empty pep talk. I am not advocating the alleged "power of positive thinking." Sometimes thinking in an overly positive way about something is even more irrational than being negative about it, depending upon the circumstances.

If I lose my leg in an accident, no amount of positive thinking will make it grow back. Even so, regardless of my feelings to the contrary, it doesn't mean that my life is over, either. The truth of such a tragic circumstance would be that I would have a very long, hard road ahead of me. Yet even in the face of such a great trial, if I would cling to God and faithfully do the exercises my physical and occupational therapists give me to do, I could learn how to have a full and abundant life that would be a testament to both the strength of the human spirit and the glory of God—with whom I could accomplish all things.

The point is that regardless of what I am facing, I am obliged to respond to it in a way that leads me, step by practical step, to a more abundant life. The prominent psychoanalyst and Holocaust survivor Dr. Victor Frankl writes in his book *Man's Search for Ultimate Meaning* that we often ask, "What is the meaning of life?" But Frankl says that we have it backward. Rather, life asks of us, "What meaning will you make of me?"

I believe this is the essence of Jesus' statement that he came that we might have life and have it more abundantly. If Jesus could confront his ignominious death on a cross in such a way that it gave meaning not only to that death but to everything that happened before it and everything that has happened since, how is it that I would not be able to approach my comparatively lesser sufferings in as noble and meaningful a way? Rather than giving in to despair and asking, "Why is my life not what I hoped it would be?" we need to ask for the grace to make whatever our life presently is into the meaningful, abundant life God wants it to be. Only then will anything about life make sense.

So far, we have discussed the source of our emotions, how to identify the thoughts that cause them, how to know whether those thoughts are true, and—if not—how to respond to them effectively. There is still one more step to the process.

Have Courage and Step Out in Faith

Too many people, despite knowing what is true and right (as we have defined those terms so far), refuse to act on this knowledge until their feelings fall into line. This is a recipe for failure. Feelings always, always, always, *follow* action. In other words, even if we know what is really true and are preaching that truth to ourselves, our anxious feelings will not change until we act on that knowledge.

The woman in our example, even though she wrote down all the reasons why she should confront her husband, will still feel anxious until she actually does it. The man in our example will continue to feel ambivalence about leaving his job at least until he actually submits his resignation. The point of talking yourself through your false automatic thoughts and feelings is not so much to change the feelings (although eventually, with practice, this will happen too) so much as it is—in the early stages, at least—to provide the motivation you need to do what is healthy and godly despite what you may feel.

Over and over, Jesus told his disciples, "Be not afraid!" There comes a point when we have been given all the information and grace we will get—all we really need—but it will still not feel like enough. This is because our feelings are the most fallen part of ourselves.

Feelings are an important source of information, but they are not the most reliable. As you practice the techniques outlined in this chapter, your feelings will begin to support more consistently those thoughts and actions you determine to be healthy. (For a more thorough examination of overcoming anxiety and other emotional problems, see the book I noted earlier: *God Help Me! This Stress Is Driving Me Crazy!)*

Initially, however, the feelings must be mastered and led, like a stubborn donkey, down the path that the mind and spirit determine is the healthiest route. Eventually, the donkey will become more trustworthy as it is trained to follow the mind and spirit. But it will take consistent use of the techniques I outline in this chapter, as well as an ample amount of prayer, before this result appears.

This final stage of the exercise is the most difficult. This is the part where you have to decide to act even if your feelings are telling you not to act.

I remember being in a high school swimming class, standing at the high dive, terrified. I was only an adequate swimmer, not fabulously athletic in the first place, and not entirely comfortable with heights. And yet, knowing that my teacher had determined that I had the skills necessary to do what was now required of me, I had to fight off feelings of anxiety and all the self-doubt that overcame me as I stood at the top of the high dive platform.

Eventually, there was nothing left to do but trust that I had all I needed to succeed: the right skills and a supportive coach.

Life is filled with moments like that. I can teach you the skills you need. I can be your coach, and God can stand at the edge of the pool rooting for you. But you are the only one who can make yourself step off the diving board.

Once you have gotten to this point in the exercise, the only thing left to do is act. You have clarified the source of your emotions, you have identified what is false, you have expressed what is true. Now act.

Take the actions you identified to be the next step on the path to a more abundant life. It doesn't matter how small or large a step it is; it only matters that you take the step in faith. Have courage and act on what you believe to be true.

Remember what we said at the end of the first chapter: God believes in you. As hideously corny as that may sound, it is undeniably true. Have courage, step out in faith, and act.

An Exercise

The following exercise will help you track through your own mental roadblocks to pursuing the path down which God is calling you. Answer all the questions as completely as possible.

Setting up the situation:

1. What is the ultimate goal to which you believe God is calling you? (For example: a better marriage, a more rewarding career, a healthier family life, a new skill.)

_____

_____

_____

_____

2. What are the smaller steps that you could begin taking today that would aid you in pursuit of that goal? (For example: seek counseling, take classes, practice a specific habit or skill, get more information.)

_____

_____

_____

_____

Identifying the negative thoughts:

3. When you think about taking the initial steps identified in number 2 above, how do you feel? (Example: confident, anxious, hopeless.)

4. What thoughts are causing this emotional reaction—that is, how would you explain or justify this reaction to someone else?

_____

_____

_____

_____

Identifying false and true thoughts:

5. What you wrote in number 4 are the thoughts that are causing your emotional reactions to the steps you outlined above (in number 2). Go through the thoughts you listed in number 4. Do these thoughts encourage you to take the steps that would lead you to a more abundant life? Or do they cause you to feel anxious, paralyzed, hopeless, confused, or cut off from God?

If they seem to point you in a direction of greater clarity of the path you should take or a fuller experience of life, then these thoughts are true. You are finished. Go and act on them now.

If, on the other hand, the thoughts lead to despair, anxiety, confusion, hopelessness, or a sense of estrangement from God, others, or yourself, these thoughts are false. They represent the things Satan is whispering in your ear to distract you from your God-given mission. They are false.

So, are the thoughts you listed in number 4 true _____ (go to 7) or false _____ (go to 6)?

6. *You have identified your thoughts to be false.*

Even though these thoughts may feel true, you have intellectually recognized that, based on the fact that they do not lead you toward the experience of a more abundant life, they are false. You must confront these lies with the truth.

On a separate sheet of paper, make an honest assessment of the concerns you face and describe your best ideas for (a) beginning to take action on the steps you identified in number 2 above and (b) your motivation for taking these steps even though you feel nervous about it.

7. *Take action.*

If you have gone through this entire process, it is time to take action, even if your feelings are still somewhat troubled. As I asserted earlier, feelings, though important, are the least reliable source of information. They must be lovingly governed by the intellect, will, and spirit if they are to be healthy.

Now is the time for action. Step out in faith and begin working on the action items you described throughout this exercise. Continue to pray that God would guide your steps, but assume that your discernment is correct unless God unquestionably tells you otherwise. Pray that you will be open to hearing his voice, but continue to step out in faith on the course of action you have discerned.

As this chapter draws to a close, you have learned some basic steps for overcoming the anxiety that stands between you and taking action on the plan God has for your life.

One more potential obstacle remains, however: other people. How do you pursue the path that you firmly believe God has laid before you while, at the same time, generously responding to the concerns expressed by others—and setting respectful limits with those who would try to stop you for various reasons? We'll examine that question and more in the next chapter.

SIX

Take Others into Account

Jim, a forty-three-year-old claims adjuster, has an opportunity to go into partnership with his brother on a new business venture. Never one to fall prey to "get rich quick" schemes, Jim has proven to himself that it is a viable business idea. Between the two of them, they have developed a workable business plan and have financing lined up to launch their new enterprise.

Jim and his brother are both serious about their faith. Raised in a solid Catholic home, they can't remember a time when the Lord and the Church haven't played a significant role in their lives. All through the planning process, they continually brought their ideas to prayer. Both believe that they are making a healthy, responsible, prayerfully informed choice.

There is one major concern, however. Jim's wife, Tanya, is terrified. Her father's business went bankrupt when she was a child, and this was a source of constant pain and frustration for her mother and father. Even now, twenty-five years later, her mother and father continue to feel resentment toward each other for all the painful adjustments that had to be made after the failure of the family's business and the loss of the money that Tanya's mother brought into the marriage.

Because this issue is packed with so much personal history for Tanya, she is extremely anxious about Jim's business plans. Even though he has tried to include her in the process every step of the way, and even though—in her calmer moments—she agrees that the numbers seem to add up, she has asked him, repeatedly, not to proceed.

Jim explained to me in session:

"I love my wife, and I would do anything for her. But I really believe that this decision is best for our family, not only financially, but time-wise as well. I know this will make me more available to the family.

"I want to respect her opinion on this, but it just isn't rational. When she's calmer, she tells me that she sees what I'm saying is right, but she is so scared. I don't want to be disrespectful to her feelings—my marriage and family are the most important things to me—and I would be willing to give this up if I had to. But it just seems too good to pass up. I don't know. What is the right thing to do?"

* * *

Angela was forty-five, unmarried, and unfulfilled in her work as the produce manager at a large grocery chain store.

"All my life," she recalled, "my mother has been an anxious person, especially where I'm concerned. When I was growing up, every time I wanted to try something, she was full of gloom and doom: 'Don't run so fast!' or 'You might not make the team, and I don't want you to be disappointed,' or 'What if this, what if that?'

"I know she was trying to show me that she loved me. I'm not angry at her for it, but I've carried all that anxiety in little tapes inside my head. It has really held me back for my whole life."

Angela and I had been counseling for awhile when she decided to take the steps necessary to become a travel agent and tour guide, something she had wanted to do for years. With her new skills, she had recently begun thinking of moving to another town, a city about three hours away. There, with a larger and wealthier population, she would have more opportunities available to her in her new line of work.

Angela had been praying about this decision for several months and believed that it was the right path. But there was a hitch.

"I was afraid to tell my mother," she confessed. "I knew she would lose it, and she did. 'Where are you gonna live? What if you get mugged? What if you get raped? What are you gonna do without your family?' Yadda, yadda, yadda. One after another with the questions."

At first, Angela told me that her mother's anxious questioning simply irritated her. But later, she became nervous herself.

"I started thinking, *What will I do?* A strange town. I don't really know anyone there. I'm not sure where I could find a good parish. And even though I haven't lived at home for twenty years, I still have been back there almost every weekend.

"My mother and father are getting older now, too. Can I really move that far away now? So many questions. Even though they drive me crazy, I love my folks. How can I be sensitive to them and still have a fulfilling life? Maybe I just can't."

Jim and Angela, though very different people, were both concerned that the path down which God was leading them would lead to serious conflict in a relationship that was important to them. Often the roadblocks we face are not caused by internal conflict, but rather concerns related to things outside ourselves. A majority of those external concerns have to do with how our decisions might affect the people to whom we are closest.

This is an important issue. As Angela put it above, how can we be sensitive to the concerns and needs of those close to us while still pursuing the abundant life God calls us toward? When others object to the plans that we have prayerfully discerned, how do we respond?

Aren't We Being Selfish?

The first question that often occurs to us when others object to our plans is to ask if we are being selfish. It is a natural and good thing to pause and reflect upon the true intentions behind our actions and the effects those actions have on others. But there is a potential glitch in the process when we confuse what is good and healthy concern with an overactive sense of guilt.

People object to our plans for many different reasons, and some of those reasons are better than others. The difficulty is that our emotional reaction to their objections—a sense of guilt—tends to be the same whether or not those objections are reasonable. Because many people make decisions primarily based on their emotional reactions (which, as you saw in the last chapter, is not a terrifically healthy thing to do), these same people become paralyzed at the least objection posed by another person. This is a sure path to a lack of fulfillment.

So how do you know whether an objection is right and reasonable and should therefore be accommodated? Again, the "abundant life test" comes into play.

Would accommodating the objection of another person lead to a greater likelihood that your plans will succeed? Would it point in a direction that is actually healthier for you and your relationship with the other person? If so, then accommodating that objection would lead to a more abundant life. (That is, it would lead to greater meaning, intimacy, and virtue.) For this reason, the objection should be seriously considered, and plans should be put on hold until a way to overcome the objection has been found.

There are three kinds of objections. The first two—objections concerning success and objections concerning relationships—are reasonable. The third—objections concerning power and control—are not. Let's take a look at each type of objection.

Objections Concerning Success

Objections concerning success are expressed by a person who is genuinely concerned with our well-being and the success of our plans. Often, we don't like to hear such concerns expressed by others. But if we respond attentively to them, we will be infinitely better off.

For example, let's say that I want to start my own business. You express concern. Your objections include the following:

1. I know nothing about starting a business.

2. Sometimes businesses take time to become profitable. How will I make a living in the meantime?

3. New businesses take a lot of time. How will I be able
    to have time for my family commitments?

There may be other objections, but let's start with those.
These pass the "abundant life test," because by taking the
time to respond thoroughly to them, I have a greater chance of
achieving the joy I hope to gain by pursuing my stated goal.

If I know nothing about business, I will need either to
take some classes, to hire a consultant, or to find a partner
who will help me make my idea profitable. If I ignore this
objection, it will be at my peril. But if I take the time to
respond to it, then I have a greater chance of success.

The same is true of the second objection. I need a plan to
pay my bills while things are getting off the ground. The third
objection also serves a more abundant life because it seeks to
protect the pursuit of both intimacy and virtue. If I am sitting
on a pile of money, but have accomplished this at the cost of
my spouse and children's affection, what have I really
accomplished?

In our desperate quest to be happy, as opposed to truly
joyful, sometimes we choose to ignore prudent objections
concerning the success of a project. This problem reminds me
of *The Miser,* a hysterical farce by the French playwright Jean
Baptiste Molière. In this story, a young man wishes to wed a
young woman. But he knows that his father, the miser of the
play, will not approve of the marriage. In fact, the young man
knows that he will be disowned and cast out of his father's
home, penniless.

The young man's sister begs him to think about his
actions: "But where will you live? How will you eat?" To these
questions her brother, who does not wish his blind pursuit of

happiness to be disturbed, responds, "There you go making trouble again!"

Objections concerning success pass the "abundant life test" because they increase the likelihood that we will succeed and that our pursuits will be meaningful. It is all well and good to pursue a business dream or romantic bliss, but if that pursuit is doomed to failure by our poor planning, what is the point of it?

None of this is to say that just because it would be hard to overcome these obstacles I should not pursue the plan. In fact, I would argue that the plan is difficult only because it presents the greatest opportunity for meaningfulness, intimacy, and virtue, and therefore it should be pursued at all costs. However, the plan should not be pursued without meeting these objections first, since meeting these objections has everything to do with being able to achieve successfully my ultimate goal.

Having considered the first type of objection we encounter, let's take a look at the second category: objections that concern how the plan will affect our relationships.

Objections Concerning Relationships

Objections concerning relationships have to do with how your plans will affect the plans of others and your relationship to others. This objection is especially important to Catholics, who need to be respectful of what theologians call the *personalistic norm*. We need to take a moment to explain this term. Even though the concepts are a little heady, they are important because they will help you know the best, healthiest, most Christian responses to make when people object to your plans. I promise to keep it simple and practical.

Most people believe that the individual is the most important unit of society and that individuals should thus pursue whatever they believe is good for them, regardless of the effect their actions have on others. This belief is called *individualism,* and it is the basis of most of secular society, as well as much of secular psychology. "What's good for me and to hell with thee" is the basic theme of individualism. And though most people wouldn't put it quite that coldly, it is a cruel philosophy nevertheless.

I am sure you have all heard someone say in response to another person's impassioned objections, "I *have* to do what's best for *me* [regardless of how it is affecting you]!" This quote is a good practical example of the individualistic norm at work. A good number of marriages and children have suffered at the hands of this norm as people went off to "find themselves," pursuing their own good at the expense of the good of others.

Individualistic attitudes developed largely in reaction to an opposite but still faulty idea: a kind of fascist belief that the only thing that matters is the good of the group, even to the degree that the individual's needs must be repressed or ignored when they conflict with the good of the group. For example, literature and history are full of stories about men and women who wished to marry for love or to pursue other interests, but were denied, saying, "What *you* want doesn't matter! You have to think about the good of the family!"

This kind of thinking represents a sort of "micro-fascism" that the Catholic Church emphatically rejects. While self-sacrifice for the good of others can certainly be a virtue if freely chosen, in many of his writings Pope John Paul II noted especially that this "you don't matter, only we do" ideology does violence to individuals because it forces upon them pseudo-generosity that is neither chosen freely nor in their best interest.

The Pebble and the Pond

In contrast to both of the above, *personalism* finds the golden middle ground between these two unhealthy extremes (individualism and fascism). Personalism tells us that neither the individual nor the group is the basis of society, but rather the "intimate community of persons."

So what, you ask? So this: In personalism, individuals are encouraged—even obliged—to pursue what is good for them, *so long as they do it in a manner that is consistent with the good of those around them.* Personalism recognizes that none of us lives in a vacuum. What you do affects everyone around you, like the ripples that are produced by tossing a pebble in a pond. One pebble affects the whole pond.

Because our actions have consequences that affect all the people around us, when we feel we must act in our own best interests we are, of course, obliged to act. We simply have to be prudent and always try to seek the path to our fulfillment that is most respectful to the needs of those around us. In this way, everyone's needs are met and our life, as well as the lives of those who surround us, exhibits a greater abundance of meaning, intimacy, and virtue. Personalism thus represents a way of life that seeks the best for both the individual and the community and ensures the greater success of both.

As an interesting side note, personalism is not just a quaint, Catholic point of view or a saintly moral norm. It has actually been *proven* true by, of all things, mathematics. In the movie *A Beautiful Mind,* based on the life of the American mathematician John Nash, Nash wins the Nobel Prize for proving, mathematically, that in economics, individualism doesn't work as well as what Catholics call personalism. The latter is actually a statistically superior model for the survival of society.

Personalism is the best and really the only way that individuals can look after their own best interests while protecting the relationships that are most valuable to them. Every other way of life besides the personalistic model does damage either to the individual or to the people the individual loves—which brings us back to our original point.

Objections concerning relationships, the second type of objection we hear when we are trying to do what we believe God is calling us to do, are mostly concerned with meeting this personalistic norm. In other words, the person expressing the objection is saying, "I don't know how I can help you fulfill the mission God has placed on your heart while still being faithful to the mission God has placed on mine." The good news is this: If both people have prayerfully discerned their mission using steps similar to the ones I described earlier in this book, and if they continue to pray together, then God will reveal the plan he has in his mind for fulfilling even two seemingly divergent plans.

Negotiating Goals

Practically speaking, the rule of thumb for negotiating seemingly conflicting goals is the "never negotiate the *what;* always negotiate the *how and when*" rule. I explain this rule in depth and how it relates to marriage and family life in particular in my books *For Better . . . FOREVER!* and *The Exceptional Seven Percent*. Essentially, however, here's the idea.

No one has the right to deny something that you believe God has called you to pursue (the *what* of the above rule). However, they do have a right to negotiate the *how* and the *when* that would allow *what* you want to be achieved in a manner that would be respectful to their needs.

For example, let's say you and I are married. You want to do something (something big, not just going to dinner at a restaurant I don't like, but say, going back to school or changing jobs, or something similar) that I don't understand. Moreover, it would seriously inconvenience me if you did it.

My first reaction might be to try to talk you out of that action, to tell you that you were crazy for wanting to do such and such. Assuming that you had prayed and used all the steps I outlined in the earlier chapter on discernment, however, I would be committing an offense against you. I would be acting out that "micro-fascism" I described above by asking you to repress the God-given desires of your heart for the sake of my comfort.

On the other hand, if you did that thing you wanted to do regardless of how I felt about it, you would be committing an offense against me. You would be acting out the individualism I described above by telling me that you had to be true to yourself regardless of how it affected me.

What to do? Well, instead of my trying to convince you that what you want is bad, and your trying to convince me that it's not, I have to assume that *what* you want is a good thing. I should not challenge or question it at all. However, we must both be willing to negotiate the best *how* and *when* (the means and the time frame) that would allow you to get *what* you want in a way that is also respectful of my needs.

Let's say that you want to return to school, and it will cost a lot of money. I am afraid that if you go to school, I won't be able to meet my goals for my retirement savings. So who's right? We both are.

Both are objectively good things to desire. So we will not waste our time trying to negotiate the *what*. Instead, we will respectfully discuss *how* and *when* you can return to school in a way that would not seriously jeopardize my plans for retirement.

Together, then, we might decide that if you take classes part-time instead of full-time, we will both be able to meet our goals. Or you might decide to do your course work with an online university so that we won't have to pay for child care. Or I could suggest that by cutting back on my morning latte and a few other simple conveniences, I can make up some of the difference and contribute those monies to the retirement account. Or maybe together we would decide that you will put off school for a semester. Or I will simply have to retire a year later.

Any of these options would be acceptable so long as we could both agree on them. The point is that at no time are we saying that what the other wants is silly or stupid. In fact, we are both working to overcome our personal desire to have what we want, how and when we want it. Instead, we are both being respectful to what the other wants while charitably negotiating the best way to accomplish both of our goals. This is an example of mature problem-solving at work.

Many people think that compromise is the art of negotiating a solution that makes everyone equally miserable. I disagree. If you use the "never negotiate the *what*; always negotiate the *how* and the *when*" rule, you will learn to see the other person with whom you are negotiating as the friend and ally who is helping you find the most respectful and efficient way to meet your needs. Following this rule allows you to avoid the traps of both selfish individualism and oppressive "groupism," while living out fully the personalistic norm to which Catholics are called in relationships.

Objections Concerning Power and Control

Of the three types of objections, those concerning power and control are the only unquestionably illegitimate ones. Ultimately, these objections are not concerned with helping you address problems you may have missed, or facilitating a healthy rapport and partnership between two people while both pursue what God has called them to do. Rather, those with objections to your plans in this category do so merely because they do not wish the status quo to be affected or their comfort level to be challenged.

They are not interested in negotiating the *how* or the *when*. Instead, regardless of how much you try to reason with them, they are committed to telling you what a stupid, ridiculous, inconvenient, or impractical idea you have. Failing that, they will resort to threats: "If you do that, I will have nothing to do with it." "If you do that, I will leave you." "If you do that, I will do everything I can to get in your way."

Sometimes the threats may not be spoken, but they will be just as real. For example, a boss who does not want his employee to do private consulting, but has no right to fire the employee because he has made certain to avoid conflicts of interest, may simply make the work environment unbearable. The husband who does not want his wife to go to counseling, or take a job, even though she has taken steps to inconvenience him or the family as little as possible, may pout and fuss and make the home a dark and oppressive place.

The wife who does not wish her husband to start his own business, or pursue some other new opportunity, even though he has taken care to leave plenty of time to fulfill his family obligations, may scream and accuse him of being irresponsible. And the mother who doesn't want her son to marry, even though the couple has received proper instruction and is responsible, will pout and accuse him of abandoning her.

All these are examples of how people sometimes place unreasonable expectations upon us and then become indignant, or outright abusive, when our plans get in the way of their comfort and convenience.

When you encounter such objections, I would argue that you must take three steps to make sure that you are being as reasonable as possible before proceeding further with your plans. First, you must pray. Ask God to give you the prudence and the wisdom to know whether the actions you want to take are really his will.

At this point, considering that you have been discerning this whole time, you should assume that they are God's will for you. But ask him to change your heart in some obvious way if, even at this point, you have gotten something wrong. If you do not have a peace about changing your plans even after you have prayed about it, this is a good indication that you should not change them, regardless of the resistance you are encountering.

Second, Christian charity requires that you must try to do what you can to make reasonable accommodations to this other person, even if he or she is being unreasonable. This does not mean that you must give up pursuing your plans. It simply means that you should go out of your way to make suggestions about how you could pursue those plans while minimizing any hardship or inconvenience to others.

At this point, the other person will show the true makeup of his or her heart—whether it is godly and good, or selfish and merely concerned with personal comfort. On the one hand, the other person may see that you are trying to be accommodating and, in appreciation of your gesture, offer ideas about how things might work to your mutual satisfaction. On the other hand, the other person may become more harsh and resistant, saying, "I already told you what I think. I want nothing to do with this."

You may even be accused of being selfish or manipulative and of trying to "make" the other person agree with you. And you may be stunned by this reaction, since it was not at all your intention to come across this way.

At this point, many people give up. They feel that if someone else has labeled them as selfish and manipulative, it must be so, even if they themselves can't see it. I assert that this is a lie.

The question you must ask yourself in such a situation is this: "Have I expressed a willingness to negotiate with this person and done my best to accommodate him or her while still being faithful to what I believe God is calling me to do?" If you can answer yes to this question, you are not being selfish. Rather, you are being manipulated for the sake of the other person's convenience.

Harry's Story: Branching Out

Harry, a successful real estate agent, had wanted to do consulting work for other real estate agents for a long time. He envisioned entering into the developing field of real estate coaching. He mentioned his training to other colleagues and began offering his services to those who were interested, all the while being careful not to jeopardize his primary commitment to his business partner, Mark, and the real estate office they operated together.

In fact, Harry had often invited Mark to join him in this pursuit. But Mark refused, saying that he had no interest in this aspect of the business.

Even so, when Harry started getting clients to coach, Mark became furious. He accused Harry of having divided loyalties, and he began making things difficult around the office for Harry.

Harry tried to reason with Mark, but Mark's only reply was that Harry was trying to do an "end run" around him. He couldn't believe that Harry would jeopardize their business by taking the time to pursue this new avenue. So Harry asked Mark to show him how his coaching work was affecting either Harry's performance or the business.

Mark refused, saying simply, "You know that you are being a jerk, and if you care about this partnership, you'll stick to what we do best." Mark was implicitly threatening to take his clients and leave the firm.

Harry and his wife, Charlotte, continued to pray about Harry's recent business decision. The fact is, Harry had been feeling burned out by his work in real estate for a long time. Since he had started coaching, though, he had felt as if he had rediscovered the enjoyment he used to get out of his work. Now he had found a way to take all the knowledge he had gained over the years and help others be successful in the field as well.

The more Harry and Charlotte prayed, the more they remained convinced that this was the right path to take. Harry was using his gifts more fully, he was using those gifts in a way that was helping others, and the path seemed to be leading toward a more abundant life. The more they thought about it, the more they realized that Mark, who had always been very secretive and was jealous of others' successes in the business, was probably afraid that Harry would give information to other firms about their business, or at least would give them information that would cause their firm to be diminished in some way.

Harry tried to allay these fears, but Mark was adamant. Harry, he insisted, must either stop his coaching work or start looking for a new partner. Mark said that he didn't feel the need to explain himself any further. He had made his opinion clear.

* * *

This case is an excellent example of the way people behave when they are making objections based on power or control. Harry had gone out of his way in an attempt to include and then accommodate Mark, but Mark had his own agenda. This would have been fine if he had been willing to articulate that agenda to Harry; then perhaps they could have negotiated the *how* and the *when* as I described earlier in this chapter.

But Mark did not have a rational agenda. He was merely operating out of fear and anger. Somehow, he felt threatened by Harry's actions, but he was unwilling or unable to explain why. Instead, he attempted to—in essence—bully Harry out of pursuing the course that Harry felt was best for his own professional development, a course Harry and his wife had prayerfully discerned that God wanted him to take.

To give in to someone who is taking this approach with you is akin to idolatry. Let me explain. When we believe in our hearts that God is calling us to act in a certain way, then we are obliged to act. Period.

Granted, we must attempt to act in a manner that is respectful of those around us. But if those others are unwilling to work with us as we try to accommodate their needs, and merely respond to us instead with emotional, irrational bullying, then to give in to this bullying is to place their comfort—and our fear of losing the relationship—over the call God has placed in our hearts. That action, placing another relationship over the call God has asked us to take up, is idolatry.

C.S. Lewis actually addressed this very point once in his book *The Four Loves*. In it, he quotes the words of Jesus: "If any one comes to me and does not hate his own father and mother and wife and . . . even his own life, he cannot be my disciple" (Lk 14:26). Lewis writes: "We must turn down or disqualify our nearest and dearest when they come between us and our obedience to God. Heaven knows, it will seem to them sufficiently like hatred. We must not act on the pity we feel; we must be blind to tears and deaf to pleadings."

This brings us to the third step that must be taken in response to the irrational objections of others: You must act. Assuming that throughout the process you have been praying and discerning, inviting the other person to work with you, or failing that, attempting to accommodate him or her the best you can, it is time to act. In the face of your action, the person who was objecting based on power and control issues may howl and scream. Even so, you cannot let yourself be swayed.

If, at some point, that person is able to articulate simple ways that you could pursue the course God has laid out before you with less inconvenience to him or her, then by all means, you should try your best to accommodate. But you should do it only to the degree that it does not stop you from acting on your plan.

Becoming a Catalyst for Change

Melinda, married to Frank for fifteen years, was desperate. He had a terrible temper and had refused for years to do anything about it. She had often asked him to go to counseling—at first, for his own sake, and then for the sake of their marriage—but he had always refused.

She had never followed through on her own, because she had wanted to respect Frank's wishes to "work it out on their own." Eventually, however, it had become too much for her. So she prayed and sought the counsel of her pastor, who told her that she needed to seek counseling to get through this situation. The more she prayed, the more she was convinced that making an appointment with a faithful counselor was the thing to do.

Frank was furious. He didn't want some stranger knowing their dirty laundry. He accused Melinda of wanting to blab their problems to anyone and everyone. He told her that she obviously didn't love him, because if she did, she would have more respect for his feelings and opinions on the matter.

Melinda had succumbed to these kinds of words for years, but through the grace of God, she was able to resist them this time. She called me to start individual telephone counseling with the hopes that Frank would join us at a later point. At the least, she hoped that she could learn how to change things without his help if necessary.

* * *

Taking action as Melinda did takes a lot of courage and fortitude, which, if a path is correctly discerned, can be exactly the point. Remember, God calls us on toward greater fulfillment not so much so we can pursue happiness, but so that we can grow in virtue. Fortitude is one of those virtues.

When we can stand in the face of adversity and follow God's plan for our lives, even—as a last resort—risking those relationships that are nearest to our heart for the sake of pursuing that path, we do grow in fortitude. We are exercising the kind of faithfulness that God sometimes asks of us.

In doing so, despite their complaints, we are actually sharing an important witness to the people who are objecting to our actions. Very often, if it is done charitably, and if there really is any godliness at all in the heart of those objecting, our actions can be the catalyst that forces them out of the comfort to which they have been clinging. It can require them to take up the cross God has been calling them to carry for years—a cross they have been able to avoid successfully because there was no one pushing them to carry it.

In the case of Melinda and Frank, Frank continued to object to her counseling for several weeks into our sessions. In the meantime, I worked with Melinda to help her discover charitable but effective ways to challenge Frank's unacceptable behavior toward her. About six weeks into my work with Melinda, they had a huge argument, but this time, Melinda was able to keep her cool.

For years, Frank had blamed her for his outbursts, saying, "If you hadn't said that, I wouldn't have lost it" or "The only reason I got so upset was that you . . ."

This time, though, Melinda was able to stay in control of herself. In spite of her restraint, Frank still lost control of his temper. It made him face the fact that there was no one to blame but himself for his behavior. He joined us in our session the following week.

Melinda's courage to move ahead despite Frank's anger and threats proved to be the door through which God poured his grace, not only to save this marriage, but to allow it to prosper. Despite a rough start to our counseling, Frank became an active participant in our sessions. Through our work together, Frank and Melinda were able to achieve a level of intimacy that had been impossible before.

Nevertheless, it took Melinda's willingness, first to discern well and then to follow that discernment, no matter what the potential cost, to make the necessary change possible. Her courage to pursue greater virtue, intimacy, and meaning in her marriage allowed both Frank and her to have the marriage God wanted them to have.

God knows the path we must take to reach the abundant life we are seeking. But we have to trust him to achieve that goal. Sometimes he will challenge us to act even over the strenuous objections of others; often he will ask us to act even in the face of serious adversity.

The Next Step

Over the last several chapters, we have examined the necessary steps to discovering and fulfilling the plan for our lives regardless of our starting point. Using the acronym FAITH, we have seen how to *follow* rules of healthy discernment, *act* even when we doubt, *investigate* the causes of our anxiety, and in this chapter, *take* others into account.

In the next chapter, we will examine the last point to achieving the mission God has for your life: *Hold on* through adversity.

SEVEN

Hold On Through Adversity

Amanda was a telephone counseling client through the Pastoral Solutions Institute. She was forty-one years old, unmarried, and dissatisfied with her job as an accountant for a local waste disposal company. She felt that her life was boring and unfulfilling. Several times she had thought about trying something else, anything else. But the ideas she came up with never seemed to work out.

"I love crafting," she said. "Once, I purchased a booth in a consignment store. My things were selling very well, and I started thinking, *Wouldn't it be great if I could make a living at this? I could do craft shows, teach classes, maybe have my work placed in a catalog or two.*

"But then the woman who owned the store called to tell me she was being forced to close. Just one more nail in my coffin. Every time I try to do something positive in my life, something I think would give me some real satisfaction, it falls apart."

I asked her why she gave up. If her work was selling so well, why not try another store?

"I figured God must not want me to do it if he would go to all that trouble to shut me down. Maybe he just doesn't want me to be happy. Maybe I'm just supposed to offer up my misery and disappointment for some greater spiritual good. God knows I've had enough of them."

* * *

Jared, thirty-nine, was divorced from his wife of eleven years. She had had an affair with a man at her office that had gone on for several months before he found out. By the time someone sent him an anonymous letter informing him of the affair so he could confront his wife, she had already decided to give up on the marriage. She got primary custody of his three children; he got the older car and the right to visit every other weekend.

Understandably, Jared was crushed. It took him almost two years before he was willing to consider dating again. At last, he fell in love with a woman at church who was also divorced. They had been dating for six months when she surprised him by announcing that, even though she felt very strongly for him, she and her ex-husband had been talking a lot lately and had decided to try to reconcile.

This just about did Jared in. If he was crushed before, he was devastated now. Though he was successful in his work, he was a sensitive man who had always valued marriage and family life. He had always felt called to marriage and was furious at God for, as he put it, "leading me on all these years."

At the point when he began counseling with me, Jared had sworn off relationships.

"I just don't think God wants me to be married," he concluded. "I always thought I was cut out for marriage and family life. Other guys couldn't care less if they ever got married; all they want is the kind of success I've found professionally.

"I'm exactly the opposite. I would give it all up if that's what it took to find a good woman and have a family to come home to. But I think maybe I've been mistaken."

I asked Jared what made him think he had incorrectly discerned what he had thought was his call to marriage. He looked at me, his expression giving away the fact that he wondered whether I was really that stupid. He said, "Just look at my life, Greg. I think that if God really wanted me to be married, it would be a little easier than this, no?"

Shouldn't It Be Easy?

It's a common belief: If God wants us to do something, there shouldn't be any struggle. Or at least there shouldn't be too much of a struggle. Most people think that when God gives us his marching orders, he sends his angels ahead to clear our path of the most challenging obstacles. All that is left to us, then, is to get over our own internal struggle with anxiety and self-doubt so we can charge on through the wide-open, resistance-free swath the heavenly host has cut through the jungle that formerly stood between us and our God-given goal.

Would that this were so. It is true that Scripture says that we can do all things through Christ, who strengthens us (see Phil 4:13). But Scripture never says it will be easy.

Jesus does not say, "Put on the wings of my grace and follow me." Rather, he says, *"Take up your cross* and follow me"* (see Mk 8:34). While there are many more similar passages of Scripture we could pair, by simply combining these two we can get God's message: We can accomplish many great things through Christ, but it will not come without a struggle.

We don't like that message, though. I speak from experience here; I don't like the struggle. We forget to keep our eyes on the prize, to remember that a resurrection comes after the cross.

Instead, we start out with our eyes on the plan God has given us, and then, like Peter walking on the water, we become terrified at the first wave that laps at our shins.

"Wait a minute!" we say. "The water" isn't supposed to be coming up *that* high! Maybe I just *thought* Jesus was waving at me to come. Maybe he was just *fanning* himself, and I jumped out of the boat in that stupid, overly eager way of mine.

"If God *really* wanted me to walk on the water, I would be walking *on* the water, not getting knocked around and splashed like this, waves practically whacking me in the knees. Boy, I really blew this one. I hope I can make it back into the boat before it's too late."

Just like Peter, we falter. We fall, and then we convince ourselves that our call was false. We climb back into the boat, take our seat, and tell ourselves that we have learned our lesson: Only foolish people get out of the boat. The wise people wait for the Lord to come and get them if he really wants them.

How wrong we are. As I have said throughout this book, when God tells us to pursue a particular life path, we think it is because that path will make us happy—and ultimately, of course, it will. But the larger point, the point we always seem to forget, is that God is using that goal, that carrot, if you will, to provide the motivation we need to pursue the intimacy, meaning, and virtue that lead to fullness and joy.

Yet intimacy, meaning, and virtue do not come easily—*by definition*. To achieve any of these things, we must challenge our comfort constantly, embrace and overcome our fears of vulnerability and pride, and be willing to face down dragons ten thousand times bigger than we are. We will be able to do it, through Christ who strengthens us. But it will not be easy.

We think we are on the right path when the doors just fly open and the dragons mysteriously fall down dead at our feet—and sometimes they do. But more often, that kind of path is not so much God's path as it is the path of least resistance. It is the wide and smoothly paved path that Satan has laid for us should we not have the courage to walk the steep, narrow, and winding path that God calls us down.

How can we tell the difference? Again, we turn to the "abundant life test." The only two questions I have to concern myself with are these: Am I doing my best to seek God's will and remain open to whatever he calls me to do? Does this path that I believe I have been called to walk lead to a more abundant life of meaning, intimacy, or virtue?

If I can answer yes to these questions, however hesitantly or reluctantly, I can know—repeat, *know*—that I am on the right path. Moreover, I can be sure that whatever resistance I encounter along that path can be overcome with Christ's grace, if I exercise fortitude and courage through the storm.

Two Journeys at Sea

Since we are talking about storms, allow me to use a metaphor. Imagine two captains ordered to take their ships to a distant port.

Along the way, the first captain encounters all sorts of obstacles. He gets caught in the doldrums, and his ship lies still for weeks. He is buffeted by storms. He realizes that his charts are not completely reliable, and his compass falls overboard. From time to time, he encounters huge sea creatures, whales and such, that terrify his superstitious crew.

Each time he encounters such an obstacle, instead of pressing on he adjusts course and takes steps to make the journey easier. He tells himself he does this "for the sake of the crew's morale."

In the doldrums, to prevent his crew from despairing, he throws a huge feast, for which the crew is grateful, but which uses up supplies at a furious pace. When the storms come, he panics, lashes the helm, and goes down below, letting the storm take him along. When he can no longer count on his charts and compass, he navigates by the stars only so far as the nearest land, and he hugs the coastline as much as possible thereafter. When he encounters the sea creatures, he guides the ship in the opposite direction.

Eventually, this captain runs out of supplies. He is desperate and sick of being at sea. He puts in at the nearest port, a failure, but he gives thanks to God that he is alive. "At least we made it through in one piece," he says as he and his crew live out the rest of their days in a desolate land far from their original destination. Lost, hopeless, beaten, but "surviving."

The second captain encounters all the same obstacles, but his *attitude* is different. Constantly, he prays for wisdom and courage, and he keeps his destination in mind.

In the doldrums, he rations his resources carefully and orders his crew to begin rowing. In the storm, he stays topside despite the high winds and the heavy rains, guiding the ship through the storm. When his charts and compass are lost to him, he carefully navigates by the stars, plotting a new course toward his ultimate destination. When he encounters the sea creatures, he cautiously stays his course.

Eventually, tired, worn, but wiser and stronger, he reaches port and receives the prize that awaits him.

Which captain are you like?

Life: The Incredible Journey

You might say that my little fairy tale is fine for what it is, but that isn't the way it is in real life. I would disagree. In fact, this story calls to mind the dramatic journey of Earnest Shackleton.

Attempting to plot a course through Antarctica, Shackleton and his crew of thirty became locked in ice. After several months of being stranded and adrift on an ice floe, his ship was crushed by the ice that encased it. He and his crew had nothing left to do but attempt to cross to land on foot.

For several days they walked, hauling two lifeboats that contained their supplies and weighed a ton each. But when they checked their sextant, it showed that while they had been walking forward, the ice had been floating backward. So they were further back than when they had started walking.

Next, they attempted a hundred-mile journey by lifeboat, through stormy seas, to the remote, unpopulated Elephant Island. Shackleton knew that they would never be found on such a desolate spot. So he was forced to leave behind the majority of his men and supplies and set out in one of the two lifeboats with four others.

They made an insane, seventeen-day, eight-hundred-mile sail in open, storm-tossed, freezing seas to a whaling station on South Georgia Island. During that journey, the weather was so terrible that they were able to take their position on only four occasions. Finally, they made the island.

It was the *wrong side* of the island. With enough food for only three days remaining, they pounded screws through the worn-out soles of their shoes for traction and attempted a crossing over the unmapped, ice-bound mountains that lay between them and the whaling station. Three days later, spent, starving, and frostbitten, Shackleton and his men arrived at their destination.

Immediately, the captain made plans to return personally to claim the men he had been forced to leave behind. Because of his determination and courage in the face of unmerciful, relentless hardship, *every single man* that began the journey with him made it home alive. For Shackleton, there was simply no other option; the cost of failure was too high. To give up meant to lose his life and the lives of his men.

We may marvel at people like Shackleton, men and women of uncommon courage who triumph against ridiculous and cruel odds. But every single Christian is called to exactly the same kind of mission. We are called by God to embark on an incredible journey: life. (And that's a journey, incidentally, that ultimately proved more daunting to Shackleton than the ice of the Antarctic.)

We *will* encounter seemingly insurmountable odds. There *will* be many points along the way when it would be easier to give up. But the cost of failure is too high for us as well.

What are the stakes? Nothing less than your life, and the lives of the whole Christian community looking to you for signs of hope and the strength to persevere in their own mission. Both of these hang in the balance of every decision we make.

Will we underestimate God's grace and providence through adversity? Will we take the path of least resistance or the path to victory? Will we sell out for the sake of our comfort and morale? Or will we press on through all manner of unfair trials and unrelentingly cruel adversities, so we can bear witness to all the world of the wonders God can work through such simple, stupid, fearful, broken creatures as ourselves?

The answer for the Christian is clear. Like St. Paul, we must *press on* in running the race with our eyes firmly set on the Lord, who inspires and perfects our faith. We must fight the good fight, with all that we are, until the day we have won the crown of salvation (see Phil 3:12-15; Heb 12:1-2; 2 Tm 4:7-8).

For the Christian, a safe life is not an option. Failure is not an option. We must press on toward the abundant life in this world—and the next.

Upon *This* Rock? You've Got to Be Kidding

God love him, the apostle Peter was an impulsive, cowardly, bumbling fool. This is the man whom Jesus once called "a satan," the man who nearly drowned jumping out of the boat when Christ called him. The man who cut off the ear of a servant at Gethsemane. The man who denied Christ three times. The man who, according to tradition, tried to flee when the soldiers were coming for him, only to be stopped at the last minute by a vision of Christ chastising him with the words *"Quo vadis?"*—Latin for "Where do you think *you're* going?"

And yet it was this very same impulsive, cowardly, bumbling fool to whom Christ said, "You are Peter ("Rock"), and on this rock I will build my church" (Mt 16:18). Why? What possible qualities did Peter have that could justify such a gift?

In short, Peter was a man of action, a passionate man, a man who was not afraid of being thought a fool, or of failure, or of speaking his mind even when he would be criticized or ostracized. Peter was a man of passion. A political zealot before he met the Lord, for all his fickleness, Peter possessed deeply held convictions for which, in his better moments, he was willing to die if necessary.

In short, Peter was the living, breathing example of the kind of person Jesus told us all to become through the parable of the talents: people who may not think we have been given much, but who are willing to use what we have been given fully and passionately in service of the Lord and others. Peter was the kind of man who would either, on his own, have been a spectacular failure, or with God's help, a phenomenal success— a witness for all generations to come. For *God's* sake, Peter was willing to be either, and it pleased God to make him both.

That is what each one of us is called to be as well. We must have the attitude that we will take what little we have been given and use it fully and passionately, not for the sake of our own comfort and quietude (which is, incidentally, the deadly sin of sloth) but in the service of God and his glory. Each one of us is called either to live a stellar life or to die trying.

This does not necessarily mean that we are called to do glamorous things with our life. But whatever we do, no matter how menial it may seem to others, we must do it in a way that distinguishes us, not for our own sake, but for the glory of God. That is what it is to be a saint: to do both small and great things, but to do them in a stellar, abundant, passionate way that leads others to Christ—to live in a way that says you will either live a life blazing with God's glory or go out in a blaze of glory for God. Either way, your life will not go unnoticed; your witness will not go unheard.

All Christians are called to live in a manner that forces non-Christians to look at them and say, "Good heavens, are you insane? Why would you be willing to pursue meaning to *that* degree, to risk everything for *that much* intimacy, to gamble all of your comfort on the pursuit of *that much* virtue? Why can't you just be satisfied with what the rest of us have? Why do you have to work so hard?"

In exchange for this single-minded, insane devotion, God promises us that we will win the crown. It will not necessarily be a crown of wealth and fame, but it will be a crown that carries with it a life full of meaning, intimacy, virtue, and therefore joy. It will be an abundant life, and we will be happy to have lived it.

A Treehouse for God

But such a life does not come easily, and that is the point of this chapter. Those of you who think that the plan God gives you should unfold before you as you waltz through life, that the mission God has given you, if it is truly from God, will magically be actualized all by itself, have been sadly, tragically misled. If it were going to be easy, God would not have had to send his only Son to die on a cross to save us and inspire us to take up our cross and follow him.

No. The fact is that God charges you with success, but Satan does not want you to succeed. This fallen, evil-choked world resists God's plan with all its might. If you fulfill God's plan, it will only be over evil's dead body, and that is a monster that does not die easily.

Several years ago, I built my children a treehouse. Not being much of a carpenter (but hoping to make up in heart what I lack in skill—the story of my life), I was disturbed to find that the frame for the back wall was not completely square. So I had to hang in an extremely awkward position, fifteen feet up, forcing the wall into shape with my foot, my knee, and my shoulder, while I held a hammer in one hand, a nail in the other (and several more in my teeth), to fix the wall in place to the platform and sidewall.

What's my point? Simply this: Like my treehouse, in fact, much, much more so than my treehouse, the world is not entirely square, either. Sin has knocked it out of joint. (As

Hamlet said: 'Time is out of joint/ O cursed spite / that ever was I born to set it right.")

Nevertheless, God creates each one of us to hold up one corner of the kingdom he is building, to force it back into the shape he originally intended it to be. Hanging in space, clinging desperately to the tools the Great Carpenter has given us, we hold on for dear life, forcing the corners of our piece of that kingdom into place while it fights back with all its might.

Does anything about this sound easy to you? No. Rewarding, certainly. Invigorating, absolutely. Exciting, definitely. But easy? Not in the least.

I want to tell you something. If you feel unfulfilled, that simply means that you are not living enough on the edge. Am I suggesting that you should take up some extreme sport like *full-contact motocross croquet?* Of course not. But I am saying that you are probably living a life that is too safe, too focused on remaining comfortable and being conventional. A life lived too aloof from others.

There is no way to feel unfulfilled if you are truly and completely engaged in meaningful work, deeply intimate relationships, and a passionately held value system. Likewise, if you don't think your work is meaningful, or your relationships are intimate, or your life is virtuous, look no further than the mirror for your explanation of why. Don't blame anybody else. You are responsible for the life you currently have, and more to the point, the life you will have.

Don't get upset. I am not blaming you for your circumstances. I am charging you with the responsibility of living your life fully. But as you well know, a full life does not come easily.

Can I Get a Witness?

I have always tried to live according to the principles I am setting forth in this book. It has led me down some very odd paths. But having followed these steps since my childhood, I am in the enviable position of being able to say that while my life is far from being over, or complete, or easy, everything I have been through and am going through makes sense to me. I want to share a bit of my story to illustrate my point that just because something is God's will does not make it easy.

For several years, I had believed in my heart that God wanted me to start the Pastoral Solutions Institute. But to be honest, I resisted it somewhat. I always kept it in the back of my mind, and I sort of halfheartedly moved toward the idea. But I was not pursuing the work God had placed on my heart with any real intention or vigor.

At the time, I was in a small but profitable private practice and, to smooth out the ups and downs of my private work, I was a consulting therapist for a local psychiatrist who ran a private mental health clinic. The arrangement was lucrative and the work—which largely consisted of supervising the progress of the chronically mentally ill patients who lived in several area group homes—was rewarding, though not terribly challenging.

Even so, I knew God wanted me to found an organization to provide tele-counseling and other resources to Catholics who were searching for ways to apply their faith to the tough marriage, family, and personal problems they were encountering. I just didn't know how badly he wanted me to do it, and how soon.

One day, I received a call from the psychiatrist's secretary telling me that I should not come in. Apparently, the office had been raided by the FBI, who had been investigating the psychiatrist for insurance fraud. During the investigation, all payments to the agency from various insurers were stopped, and since I earned a percentage of collected billings, my salary dried up as well.

To make matters worse, my wife became deathly ill at the same time. We were being attacked from all sides. I knew God wanted me to start the Institute, but how could I with everything that was going on?

For a while, I thought that perhaps I should even close my practice and take a job somewhere that would simplify life and get us good health benefits. It was a logical option. But it certainly did not lead us toward greater meaning or intimacy or virtue, since the idea was born of a sense of despair, resignation, and hopelessness.

My wife and I continued to pray, however, and together we felt the Lord continue to lead us toward the direction of founding the Institute. So, with no money, no real plan, and little certainty about her health, we did.

The first year was extremely difficult. In addition to my wife's severe health problems (she was able to get out of bed for only a few hours every day), we had very little money. I remember that a carnival came to town and set up shop in the parking lot of the local grocery store. That year, we had to explain to our children that we could not afford to take them because we didn't have twenty dollars to spare.

Even so, God in his mercy gave us the grace we needed to remain faithful through trial and, in a short time, he allowed the Institute to prosper. God has used this organization, young as it is, to touch the lives of literally tens of thousands of Catholics worldwide. Likewise, in these years, God has led us to find good people who could advise us on how to control the symptoms of my wife's illness. Even though she has the occasional acute flare-up, she is able to lead a comparatively healthy and full life.

My point is this: The path we took was not the easy, safe, comfortable one. Please don't misunderstand me; I do not deserve any credit for any of this, for as Jesus said, "Does [the master] thank the servant because he did what was commanded?" (Lk. 17:9). The Institute's founding is a remarkable story, but not so much because of anything I, or my wife, or any of the people who work with us have done, as it is a testament to God's faithfulness and providence.

The larger point is that even though the Institute is successful now, there was nothing logical or easy about starting it. Still, we knew it was God's will for several reasons.

First, it was the path to greater meaning in our lives. Second, it resulted in greater intimacy, both because it allowed us to use our gifts more fully for the glory of God and because it allowed my wife and me to work more closely together. Finally, it led to greater virtue in that it called us to exercise trust, patience, fortitude, and a host of other spiritual qualities. Because of this, we knew it was the right path, even though it was an extremely trying and difficult path.

The Red Herring of Success

While it is wonderful news that the Institute has been so successful, if it was unsuccessful, or not as successful, that would not mean it was not God's will.

If our efforts had failed, or if we were still struggling to get it off the ground, we would still know that it was God's will. Why? Because it was and remains for us the best path at the time for using our gifts more fully (pursuing greater meaning), building greater intimacy, and fostering further virtue. As long as my wife and I discerned that this enterprise was our best option for meeting those three ends, we would be obliged to continue our efforts unless or until a better option to pursue those goals presented itself.

It is an easy and even understandable temptation to think that success would be confirmation of God's will. But it is not. Hitler's Third Reich was an unquestionable "success" (as far as Hitler was concerned, anyway), but it was certainly not God's will for the people of Germany or the world.

Likewise, there are many worthwhile enterprises that struggle for years before finding some measure of stability—if ever. Why? Because God is not concerned with success. He is concerned with the furthering of meaning, intimacy, and virtue.

I continue to beat this drum at the risk of redundancy because it is not easy to get this idea through our very thick skulls. We are brainwashed to think that ease and success are the measures by which we know God's will is being fulfilled, but they are not. To live an abundant life does not necessarily mean living a wealthy life, or a successful life, and it certainly does not mean living an easy or comfy life.

Rather, an abundant life is a life in which every activity you are engaged in is dripping with meaning; fully utilizes your gifts and talents for the glory of God and the good of others; draws you into deeper relationship with those around you; and inspires you to be a better man or woman, a more useful tool in the hand of the Lord. If you could say this about your life—regardless of the financial success or fame you achieve, the ease or comfort you enjoy, or even the lack of all these things—you would experience your life as abundant. You would be fulfilled.

Restless Is the Heart

Isn't that what we all really want? The fame we pursue, the money we crave, all the comfort we desire—isn't it really just a longing for the abundance I am describing here? As we noted earlier, St. Augustine once said, "Our hearts are restless, O God, until they find their rest in you." To apply what I am describing in this book is to put Augustine's prayer into practice.

But if spiritual abundance is the thing we all really crave, then why are we so quick to give up on it? Because we forget that we must hold on through trials. We experience hardship and we doubt that we have discerned God's will correctly. It takes longer than we think it should, or it is more difficult than we expected it would be, so we assume that we got it wrong somehow.

As challenging as the situation may be, we must not judge God's will by the world's standards of ease and success. As Scripture says, his ways are high above our ways (see Is 55:9). We must use the steps outlined earlier in this book to discern what is the most meaningful, intimate, and virtuous path we can walk, then stay on that path no matter what.

When I was a child, I used to walk to school fairly often (uphill, both ways!). Toward the end of the walk, there was a very long hill on which the school sat. I remember standing at the bottom of the hill, looking at the school way up top.

As long as I kept looking at the school and how much farther I had to go, the trip uphill seemed to last forever, and I felt every step. But one day I had the idea just to look down at my feet so that I could see just where I was, and the next step, but not how far I had come or how far I had yet to go.

Taking this approach, I practically bumped my head into the school before I knew it.

Life is an uphill climb. Do not allow yourself to be discouraged by the distance between you and the goal God is asking you to pursue. Be sure that you are on the right path in the first place, then keep your eyes on your feet and the next step, and keep walking. You will be surprised at the distance God helps you cover when you keep your mind on your ultimate destination and you aren't counting every inch of every mile.

* * *

Beverly, thirty-five, wanted to be a teacher. She loved to read, she loved children, and she loved to learn. Unfortunately, she had let her family talk her out of this dream when she first attended college. She majored in business instead and worked for several years in the marketing department of a plastics manufacturing company.

At age thirty, she married Michael, and they had two children over the following four years. When her children were closer to school age, she began revisiting her dream of being a teacher. She and her husband prayed and discussed the best way to pursue this goal.

Throughout the discernment process, she continued to feel called by God to become a teacher. She enrolled in classes, but soon afterward she developed a seizure disorder that was initially unresponsive to medication. Between the illness and the medical testing that followed, she was forced to withdraw from classes halfway through her first semester.

"I was devastated," Beverly recalled. "I didn't understand why God would let this happen to me. Was wanting to teach such a terrible thing? I really wanted this, and every time I prayed, it was as if I felt in my heart that he kept saying to me, 'Teach my children.'

"I couldn't understand it, but I knew that this call on my heart wouldn't go away. God wanted me to teach, and it was my job to figure out a way to make that happen. I was sure of it."

Around this time, she read an article in a national magazine on the growing popularity of homeschooling. "At first I thought it was crazy," she said. "But the more I thought and prayed about it, the more I saw it as a way I could keep the strong relationship I wanted with my kids and get my feet wet in teaching while I got my medical situation under control."

At this point, her plan was to teach the children at home through kindergarten and first grade and then enroll the children in school. Assuming that her health had improved, she would take up her classes again.

"People told me I was crazy. The doctors were concerned that the stress of teaching my children at home would aggravate the disorder. My mother just thought I was from another planet, and some of my friends started treating me as if I had fallen off the stupid truck.

"But I knew that God was calling me to teach, and I wasn't about to waste years sitting around being a patient until I could do it. I asked God to help keep me strong enough at least to teach my children. I just told him that I would take it one step at a time and trust that he would show me what to do when the time came."

It was a tough road. Some days she wasn't sure how much longer she could keep it up. "I almost decided to quit about a hundred times," she said, "but I kept asking myself, what are my choices? If I stop teaching, will I sit around staring at the walls waiting for my next PET scan? I don't think so.

"I think that probably would have been the saner thing to do. But even though homeschooling was hard, I was loving it.

My kids and I were closer than ever, and they were blowing me away with how well they were learning. I was getting a rush out of teaching. I was teaching! It was all too worthwhile to give up."

Eventually, Beverly responded to treatment. But she found that while she had remained faithful to God's call to teach his children, the form had changed. "I'm not sure if I will ever go back to school for my teaching degree. I can imagine it some day, but I enjoy what I am doing so much that I don't see any reason to change."

Right now, Beverly's plan is to take each year as it comes and evaluate whether the homeschooling option continues to work for her and her children. But her perseverance through trial is paying off in the form of a fuller use of her gifts, greater intimacy in her family, and virtues such as fortitude, love, and courage in spades. Can there be any doubt that Beverly is doing God's will for her life?

* * *

Throughout this chapter, I have attempted to dispel the myths that the mission God gives you for your life must happen easily or even be successful according to the world's standards. You have seen that discerning the proper path at the outset, and faithful prayer and continued discernment combined with perseverance, lead to the abundant life that comes from pursuing meaning, intimacy, and virtue.

Most of this book has concerned itself with teaching you how to overcome the self-imposed obstacles that cause you to be frustrated and disappointed with your life. Still, a great deal of disappointment comes from outside you. As the aphorism says, "Man makes plans, and God laughs."

This chapter, about holding on when obstacles present themselves, proves to be a good segue for the topic of dealing with those things such as sickness, tragedy, and other unexpected calamities that are totally beyond our means to control. How can we respond to even the worst of circumstances in a manner that allows us to find and follow the light of Christ to the resurrection that comes after the cross? The next chapter will examine this question and much more.

PART THREE
FURTHER STEPS

EIGHT

Conclusion: Moving from Suffering to Surrender

Marguerite was devastated. Widowed at thirty-seven, and the mother of three, she felt numb. Tearfully, she told me in session, "I always imagined us retired someday, traveling or visiting with our grandkids. I never imagined this. I don't know what I'm supposed to do."

* * *

Al, forty-nine, couldn't believe it. He had been one of the lucky ones. For twenty years, he had kept his job at the steel mill. Through layoffs and downturns, he had always managed to keep his job. He had figured that he had it made.

Now the plant was closing. Soon, he and three thousand other men and women would be looking for work.

"Where am I supposed to go? I'm almost fifty, for crying out loud. Who's going to hire me? I haven't paid off my house. I've got a kid in college. Why is God doing this to me?"

* * *

All Flannery, thirty-six, ever wanted was to have children, to be a mother. Despite years of trying, she and her husband, Phil, were unable to conceive. Tests showed that she had several problems with her fallopian tubes and her cervix—a combination that would prevent her from sustaining a pregnancy, if by some miracle she was able to get pregnant in the first place. After visits to several specialists, it was clear there was nothing that could be done.

"I don't understand," she said. "This is all I ever wanted to do. I just feel so hopeless."

* * *

Bad things happen. Tragedy strikes. Hopes are demolished, and often, there is nothing we can do to stop it.

Up until now, we have been discussing how we get in our own way, how erroneous beliefs, irrational thoughts, and ill-advised actions cause us to pursue false paths that lead to blind alleys. But sometimes—in fact, often—the reasons for our frustration and disappointment in life are completely beyond our control. We do all the right things, and then things fall apart.

* * *

Becky and John were married for twelve years. All their friends thought they had the perfect marriage. John was a successful attorney, they were active in their parish, and they even taught the parish marriage preparation program.

All the easier to understand, then, why Becky was devastated when she found out that John was having an affair with the nineteen-year-old college girl John had found to help Becky take care of their children. But the worst was yet to come.

In the aftermath, Becky discovered that there had been several other affairs. In fact, there had been at least two other relationships lasting six months, and from the looks of it, there had probably been several one-night stands as well. After unloading all these revelations on her, John informed Becky that he was moving out so he could have time to think.

She begged him to get help for himself and the marriage. But all he would ever say was that he would think about it. If she tried to press him for answers, he would become angry and defensive, telling her that she was trying to "pressure him" into making up his mind, and she "had no right to be so controlling."

Becky told me, "I feel as if the last twelve years of my life were some kind of joke. I don't understand. We were so good together. It just doesn't make any sense."

* * *

I hear stories like these all day long, and they never get any less shocking or painful. Hour by hour, I am charged with helping such people make sense out of their suffering, to discern the answers to questions for which there are no easy answers.

* * *

Diana, fifty, was consumed with anger, pain, grief, and anxiety. She had had a terrible childhood filled with abuse. Her first marriage, to an alcoholic, was likewise abusive, but she stayed in the relationship, largely, she said, because she had nowhere else to go. She had never graduated high school, and she couldn't go back to her parents, so she had stayed.

Eventually, her husband was killed in an industrial accident. She reported feeling guilty that the thing she felt most about this man's death was relief. "Now he couldn't be around to torture me anymore."

She took the money she received from his life insurance policy and got her G.E.D. She then took courses at the local community college and received her diploma in nursing. She got a job working for a local obstetrician.

"It was wonderful," she said. "I had my own income, my own life. For the first time, I really felt like things were going to be OK."

In fact, things were better than OK. She worked closely with Martin, the physician's assistant in the OB's office. They fell in love and married within a year. It was a wonderful marriage.

Two years into the marriage, Martin got sick. It was advanced kidney cancer, and it had metastasized to the spleen. Six months later, he died.

"Martin was the only person who ever loved me," Diana said. "He was the only person who ever made me feel special. No one else in my life *ever* cared about me. Not my parents, not my first husband. I never really knew I was worth anything until I met Martin.

"Why? Why would God do this to me? The only thing I can think is he must be punishing me for feeling glad when Jack died. Why? I didn't deserve this. Oh, God, Martin didn't deserve this. Why did God do this to us?"

Why Me?

The first question we are tempted to ask when we are suffering is *Why?* Is God punishing me? Is God trying to teach me something? Does he hate me?

As sincerely asked and understandable as these questions are, none of them are useful for helping us respond in a faithful way to suffering. God is a loving Father, dedicated to delivering us from suffering as any loving father would. Although he permits suffering to exist, for reasons that unfortunately are beyond our capacity to understand fully, our loving Father stands always ready to lead us out of our darkness, step-by-step, if we just know how to look for his light.

In general, *why* questions—at least the kind Diana was asking—do little to lead to the path God is calling us to walk down, the path that will lead us out of our pain and into the next stage of our lives. But there are questions that can reveal God's deeper plan and help set us on the right path out of even the most terrible circumstances.

Earlier we quoted Victor Frankl, an extraordinarily wise psychiatrist and survivor of the Holocaust. During World War II, Frankl was a prisoner in the concentration camps of Nazi Germany. While there, he observed his fellow inmates.

Some simply went to bed and didn't wake up. It was not so much that they were sick, though sickness was rampant in the camps. It was more that they had given up, that they had almost willed themselves to die.

Others persevered through the unspeakable misery. They watched their spouses and children murdered in the most sadistic ways before their eyes. They endured hardship that you and I could scarcely imagine. Disease, starvation, and the constant threat of death hung over them.

Nevertheless, some refused to die. They persevered. Despite everything, they survived.

Frankl writes that we often ask, "What does suffering mean?" Yet that question implies that we are passive players in the mysterious game of life, that our role is but to sit around waiting for our life to tell us what to make of it. Anyone who has ever tried this approach has never learned anything about life or suffering. They have only become more bitter, or been forced into leading a smaller and smaller life, intimidated by the incredible cruelty and seeming absurdity of it all.

God's gift to human beings of both free will and responsibility contradicts such a passive stance. The only way, said Frankl, to discern meaning even in the face of suffering is to embrace fully our will and responsibility (that is, our ability to respond to life) and become active players in the search for meaning.

In *Man's Search for Ultimate Meaning*, Frankl tells how soon after World War II a Jewish woman came to a certain doctor for an examination. She wore a bracelet made of baby teeth mounted in gold, and he noted how beautiful it was. Then the woman noted how each tooth had belonged to one of her children, and she named each daughter and son according to age.

"Nine children," she finally said, "and all of them were taken to the gas chambers."

The doctor was shocked. "How can you live with such a bracelet?" he asked.

The Jewish woman softly replied: "I am now in charge of an orphanage in Israel."

"As you see," Frankl concludes, "meaning may be squeezed out even from suffering, and that is the very reason that life remains potentially meaningful in spite of everything."

The woman in this story managed to respond to the excruciating suffering forced upon her in a way that ultimately gave her a sense of meaningfulness. Who, if not this woman, would have the right to live a quiet, uneventful life, one in which she could sit and wait to die in what peace she could manage to find somewhere far away from people and the cruelty of the world?

Yet this woman did not choose that easy path. We can almost imagine her stubborn determination, standing up in life's face, shaking her fist, and saying with every ounce of strength she can find within her being: "In spite of everything, you will be meaningful. My life will not be for nothing."

This is the only legitimate approach we can take in the face of disaster if we wish to find meaning, intimacy, virtue, and therefore, even joy, in spite of it. We must be able to stand at the gates of hell and know that through God's grace, we can prevail even against these.

The Passion of Christ

In certain circles, much is made of Christ having come to take away our suffering. These individuals quote the prophet Isaiah, who writes: "He was wounded for our transgressions, he was bruised for our iniquities; upon him was the chastisement that made us whole, and with his stripes we are healed" (Is 53:5). With this passage, certain Christians insist that Christ came to suffer—so that we wouldn't have to.

Well, it is certainly nice to think so. Would that it were true. While I am sure that these individuals are well intentioned, the fact remains that if Jesus came to take away our suffering, then he certainly did a lousy job of it. Look around. Can you doubt that suffering still exists?

I do not believe that Christ came so much to take away our suffering (though he certainly desires our deliverance from suffering) as to show us that suffering has meaning and purpose. I would submit that suffering is the temporal consequence of living in the fallen world.

Some suffering comes because the world is broken. Some suffering comes as we fight to set the world right again. But all suffering can be meaningful, and *that* is the point of Christ's Passion.

Scripture does not say, "Death, where are you?" It says, "O death, where is thy *sting?*" (1 Cor 15:55, emphasis mine). The sting of suffering, even the real pain of death, is the *seeming meaninglessness of it all.* But could anyone seriously argue that suffering has no meaning after Christ, the perfect Victim, showed us how to suffer in such a way that we can snatch victory right out of Satan's jaws?

That is how Christ's Passion brings us comfort. It does not destroy suffering, at least not in its entirety. But it shows us how to suffer well, to suffer *not just nobly, but in a way that leads us to victory.*

That leads me to the single most important question you must ask yourself in the midst of suffering. Instead of asking why, which so often leads to blind alleys and doubt, ask this question: How can I respond to this pain in a way that will make Satan sorry that he ever challenged me?

This question more than any other will help you discover the grace that God gives you to make meaning out of your suffering. This question leads you to the response you must make in answer to life's question, "What meaning will you make of *me?*" This question allows you to stand in the face of Satan, who is laughing at your pain, and snatch victory from his hands.

Isn't this exactly what Jesus did through his Passion, death, and resurrection? Christ did not desire his suffering; he asked for the cup to be taken away (see Lk 22:42). But when that was not possible, he endured the pain nobly.

More than that, Jesus used the humiliation, the pain, even his death to procure the salvation of all humankind for all eternity. Satan's crowning moment was his dethroning. When Jesus tells us to take up our cross and follow him, he is giving us a warning and a promise.

There will be crosses, there will be pain, there will be agony, and there may even be death of many kinds. But if we take up our cross and follow him, Christ will not only lead us "through the valley of the shadow of death" (Ps 23:4), he will lead us through the same opening he walked through on that first Easter morn. He will show us how to turn our cross into our glory, just as he did with his.

There will be many times in your life when you hear Satan cackling in your ears and feel his hot breath sapping you of what little strength you have left. Fine. Let him have his moment. You will suffer, you will grieve, you will ache for justice that seems as if it will never come.

But as you endure Satan's lash, the one question you must ask yourself over and over is this: When the worst of this is over, how will I live to make Satan sorry that he ever challenged me?

When my wife and I were married, we were told that we would probably not be able to have children. My wife had a medical condition that was controlled by medication, but that medication would have been hostile to a developing baby. Any pregnancy, the doctor said, would most likely kill both the child and my wife.

By a miracle, however, my wife was healed of that illness two years into our marriage. Within six months, we were pregnant. We were beside ourselves with joy and eagerly anticipated the birth of our first child. Sadly, that pregnancy ended in miscarriage.

We were devastated. So many hopes and dreams died with that pregnancy. But the loss started a chain of events in our lives with incredible ramifications. In response to that loss, and the incredible pain and betrayal we both felt, we responded as I have been encouraging you to respond throughout this book, by asking constantly: How can we live more meaningfully, intimately, and virtuously even through the pain?

Every time the pain would come—and it continued to come for several years after the miscarriage—we would pray, asking God to help us learn how we could respond to it so that we might find meaning in it all. And God showed us.

Step-by-step, he led us to the personal and professional changes we needed to make so that incredible things could happen. Everything we have now—the intimacy of our marriage, the incredibly strong relationship we have with the children God eventually gave us, the books I write and the Christian counseling ministry I do, the television and radio ministries we have—can be traced to the answers we attempted to give when life asked us, "And what meaning will you make of this?" I have no doubt that Satan is very sorry that he has picked on us, and you have no idea how much that gratifies me.

By no means was this the first or last time my wife and I have suffered in our lives. But that is not the point. The point is that each time we encounter suffering of any kind, once the worst is over and we can think straight again, the first question we ask is the one we've asked so many times before: How can we respond to this in a way that will make Satan sorry for having put us through this? Each time we ask this question, God leads us to the next thing we must do to set our corner of his world a little more right than it was before we were handed our cross.

Thinking with Grace in Mind

People are often at a loss when I first put that question to them. *How will you respond to this suffering in a way that will make Satan sorry he ever challenged you?* The world, not to mention our past experience, tells us that we are worthless, that we have nothing to give, and that our gifts are too simple to accomplish any great good in our lives.

The world would have us bury our God-given gifts and charisms because they seem so small in comparison to the demands of the world. So we must remember once more that the Scripture tells us we can do all things through Christ, who strengthens us (see Phil 4:13). Let's review the basics.

God gave you the gifts and charisms you possess, and God inserted you into this moment in time. Therefore, God must believe that you are up to the task of righting your corner of the world, no matter how difficult the task may seem at the moment. And, as Scripture says, if God is for you, who can be against you? (see Rom 8:31).

There may be times when, contrary to the popular platitude, you wonder whether God has, in fact, given you more than you can handle. Even so, never doubt that with God, you can pull deeper meaning, intimacy, and virtue—and therefore joy—out of the jaws of the deepest suffering. To do so, you must continue to challenge yourself with that question: How can I respond to this suffering in a manner that will make Satan sorry that he challenged me?

Given that God believes in us and has given us the gifts necessary to achieve meaning out of even the greatest suffering, I suggest to my clients another rule of thumb when they are confronting the pain of their lives: The degree of suffering you endure is directly proportional to the greatness to which God is calling you.

Again, we take our cue from Jesus Christ. Jesus was called to endure the sufferings of the world upon his shoulders. He who was perfect was called to face crushing humiliation, unspeakable pain, exhaustion, dehydration, blood loss, lashes, piercing with thorns and nails, exposure, and ultimately, suffocation (for that is how death by crucifixion is achieved).

What could possibly give meaning to such a horrible, grotesque death? Nothing less than the winner-take-all battle against Satan for the soul of humankind from the beginning of time and to the end of time. And that is exactly what Christ was called to do. His suffering was proportional to the greatness to which he was called.

The saints provide more examples of this "suffering endured is proportional to greatness expected" dictum. Pick a saint, virtually any saint, and you will see what I mean. Their suffering ultimately propelled them to become powerful witnesses to the glory of God. Their suffering was proportional to the greatness to which they were called. And so will yours be.

Don't get the wrong idea, however. I do not mean to imply that your suffering will call you to be great in the sense that it glorifies you, or that it necessarily leads to great wealth or fame. It may not.

What I mean is that the degree to which you suffer is the degree to which God is calling you to do great work for the good of others and the glory of God. Just as God's Son was called to do. Just as the saints were called to do before you.

When I tell people this, the reaction I often get is "Oh, great. God is calling me to be great, but I get nothing out of it. I am just a pawn in God's great game of restoring order to the world."

If this is your reaction, take heart. God is calling you to something greater than wealth or fame. He is calling you to *joy*.

What wouldn't you give if you could feel truly joyful in spite of your present pain? What wouldn't you endure to feel truly right inside, to feel, on the deepest level, that you are worthy? That your life has meaning? That God has chosen you to play an important and vital role in setting the world right again?

Called to Greatness

God calls each of us to be a saint, and as such, he calls each of us to greatness. Not the greatness that comes from pursuing wealth and fame, but the greatness that comes from pursuing meaning, intimacy, and virtue. By challenging yourself to seek the most of these three qualities you can squeeze out of your suffering, you will achieve both the greatness and the joy God has in store for you.

Often, when I first ask people the "How can you respond to your suffering in a way that will make Satan sorry that he challenged you?" question, I can hear in their voice that they are not thinking with grace in mind. The woman who lost a husband will say, "Oh, I guess I'll get a job somewhere and visit the grandkids. Hopefully I won't be too much of a bother." The man who suffers an accident says, "I'll just be glad to get through the day."

Mind you, I am not saying that there is anything wrong with these statements. And if I heard even the remotest expression of joy in the tones of voice of these individuals, I would agree that yes, this is what they are being called to. But more often, I hear no sound of the possibility of joy. Instead, I hear the strong sound of resignation in their voices.

That is exactly what Satan desires of us. He wants us to resign. He wants us to despair that we could, with God's abundant grace, derive anything truly meaningful, intimate, or virtuous.

To Satan's way of thinking, if we refuse to be crushed by our suffering, then we should be content to live a small and quiet life in which we are not a threat to anyone, least of all to him. Gently, I encourage my clients, as I now encourage you if you are confronting pain, loss, and suffering, not to let this happen to you.

The last thing a Christian should do in the face of suffering is to go quietly. Christians are called to do nothing less than rage against the evil of the world, and one of the greatest evils of the world is suffering. Sadly, in our fallen world, suffering is inescapable, but Christ's example demonstrates that suffering is not meaningless.

Done well, suffering is merely the pain we must endure as we set about the work of righting a lopsided world. If you are suffering, it simply means that God trusts that you are strong enough to join his Son and his saints in doing your part to rebuild the world according to its original purpose and plan.

If you are suffering, I want you to think big. In the face of this struggle, what is the fullest, most dramatic way you could use the gifts God has given you to work for the good of others and his glory? What would you need to do with your life that would make it possible, at some point in the future, to look back and see this pain you are currently enduring as the catalyst for the meaningfulness, intimacy, and virtue—and therefore, joy—that you seek?

Once you have the answer to that question—and no one can answer it but you—you will know the mission to which you are called. Make a promise today before God that you will either fulfill this mission or die trying. Resolve yourself to this today. For if you really wish to fulfill the purpose of your life, if you wish to be given the grace to steal joy from the clutches of pain, if you wish—at the end of your life—to hear God say those precious words, "Well done, my good and faithful servant," then this is what you must commit yourself to do.

Diana's Story

Earlier in this chapter, I shared the story of Diana, the woman whose life was filled with so much pain and loss. After the tragic death of her second husband, Diana went into a tailspin. She quit her job. She spent much of her day in bed. She refused to answer the phone or let friends see her. Her children began thinking they might have to hospitalize her for suicidal depression.

"I remember lying in bed wishing I would just die," she said. "I had nothing to live for. I wouldn't kill myself. I was too afraid to do that. But I just prayed that God would take me in my sleep. Every morning I woke up angry that I woke up.

"I didn't pray much then. I was too angry at God. But I remember saying one morning that if he wasn't going to take me, he needed to tell me what to do. I needed a reason to keep living. I needed to matter to someone."

Diana told me it was around that time that she saw a report on the national news mentioning a group called in French *Médecins Sans Frontières* (Doctors Without Borders). They were providing medical services to victims of the war in the Balkans.

"It was a miracle that I heard the report," she recalled. "I spent most of those days dozing off and on. At first it didn't mean anything to me. But my mind kept coming back to it."

The name of this organization kept coming back to her. She went to its website and became intrigued by the idea of using her nursing degree in this new and powerful way, helping victims of war and famine. She decided then and there what she needed to do.

Diana completed the organization's training and joined a medical team volunteering in Mavinga, Angola. Due to a twenty-seven-year-old civil war in that country, the people of certain sections of the region had not received any international aid in years.

"During that year," Diana told me, "I watched a lot of pain, suffering, and death. But I made a difference, too. There are babies that would not be alive today if I hadn't done this. Mothers who would not have lived to care for their children had I not been there."

Diana started to tear up. "One night, I had a dream that Martin came back to me. He whispered, 'I needed to go to let you give your gift to them.'" She paused to compose herself.

"People thought I was crazy for doing this. But it saved my life, and I know that God has a purpose for me, and I know that Martin still loves me and believes in me—he's just doing it in heaven now."

After Diana finished her one-year stint with Doctors Without Borders, she decided to return to school to pursue studies leading to her nurse practitioner certification. She now hopes to work in hospice, where she can continue to help people who are suffering: "I think I would like hospice work because there is a real focus on providing care to the whole person, including the spirit. That's not something you have the opportunity to do as much of in other specialties."

Diana used her own suffering as the catalyst for discovering how to use her gifts more fully, and in a way that is giving her life greater meaning, intimacy, and virtue. Despite her incredible pain, she was able to find dramatic ways to work for the good of others and the glory of God.

"If you had told me even a few years ago that I would be doing any of these things," she admitted, "I would have said you were crazy. I never really thought much of my gifts. I didn't really think God had given me any. Nobody ever told me I was special, that's for sure."

She added with a wink: "If God could do this much with a no-talent like me, just think what he could do with everybody else."

God Believes in You

I am sure you would agree that Diana is hardly a "no-talent." But often we cannot discover our true worth in God's plan for righting the world until we are tried by fire. Because of how she had been beaten down in her life, she could not possibly know the amazing gift that her life truly is to the world until, by suffering well, she proved to herself that with God, there was nothing she could not do. As undesirable as hardship is, when we learn how to suffer well and courageously, we learn to appreciate the incredible stuff of which we are made.

This brings us back to a point I made in the first chapter of this book. God believes in you. Never doubt it for one minute.

You do not have to believe in yourself; in fact, that would probably be foolish. On our own, we are worthless. The truth is that life is so big, so overwhelming, so trying, that we can barely get through the day on our own power, much less accomplish anything for the good of others and glory of God. With the Lord, however, all things are possible. Even you.

When you experience loss, limitation, hardship, setbacks, disease, and depression—and trust me, you will—the first, most important thing you must do is hit the floor. Get on your knees and pray this prayer.

Oh, God.

It hurts so bad. My problems are so big, so overwhelming, so painful. If it is your will, I beg you, in the name of your Son, to deliver me from my pain. I join my cry to that of Christ in the garden and I beg you, "If it is your will, let this cup pass."

But Lord, if it is not your will, then I beg you to give me strength, for I will do what you ask me to do. Just tell me what that is. Give me the courage to know how to respond to this suffering in a way that will make Satan sorry that he ever challenged me. Give me the wisdom to know what to do, so that I can hear you whispering in my ear, "Well done, my good and faithful servant."

I long for your peace and comfort. But if I cannot have that, then give me your will and your strength, so that through this, my life may become more meaningful, more intimate, more virtuous, so that I may more fully work for the good of others and your glory.

Have mercy on me God, for I am your servant. I love you. I place my trust in you. Amen.

Suffer With Christ

When we are suffering and in pain, it is good to reflect on the suffering of Christ. When I suggest this approach, many people initially think I am trying to "guilt" them out of their pain, as if I am saying, "Look how little you are suffering compared to Jesus! What do you have to complain about?" But that's not what I mean at all.

It is silly to compare our suffering to Christ's. Each person has his own work to do when it comes to rebuilding the world according to God's plan. Jesus had his task, and you have yours. We must take up *our* cross and follow Jesus, not *his* cross.

Similarly, each person will be called to endure the particular suffering that accompanies his or her mission to the world, for that is ultimately what suffering is: the pain that results from doing the work needed to set the world right. So when I suggest reflecting on the suffering of Christ, I simply mean that you must always remember that you are not suffering alone. Christ suffers alongside you. Furthermore, reflecting on the suffering of Christ allows you to follow his lead.

What do I mean? Allow me to explain.

We may feel guilty when we experience despair, anger, or sadness in the face of our pain. Still, this is a normal part of the process. It is nothing to feel guilty about.

All this means is that we are exhausted. These emotions are God-given responses that tell us that our bodies, minds, and spirits are reaching maximum capacity and in danger of overloading. It is at this point, however, that we experience the power of grace.

At the point when we recognize that we cannot do it on our own, that we have nothing left, that is the very moment when we can look down and know that it is grace, not our own feet, that is carrying us. If we can see this through the eyes of faith, it is at this moment when we most connect with the idea that God's glory is revealed in our weakness. When despair comes, we must keep walking, but we can cry out to the Lord to carry us.

When a woman is in the stage of labor called transition, the pain of labor has reached its peak. This is the stage where she wants to give up and go home: "Just stick the baby back in! I don't want to do this anymore."

But transition is also the stage of labor right before the head of the baby crowns and the child is brought into the world. Likewise, the anger, the pain, the despair you may be feeling in reaction to your suffering often come at the point when your glory is upon you.

When Jesus was on the cross, he began to pray Psalm 22, which begins, "My God, my God, why have you abandoned me?" (V.1). This prayer sounds like the very soul of despair. The Son of God is hanging on a cross, his hands and feet pierced, and he cries out in anguish to his Father, asking, in essence, "Where are you? Why have you left me here?"

From this anguished beginning, however, the psalm goes on to speak a message of hope.

> *I will tell of thy name to my brethren; in the midst of the congregation I will praise thee: You who fear the Lord, praise him! All you sons of Jacob, glorify him, and stand in awe of him, all you sons of Israel! For he has not despised or abhorred the affliction of the afflicted; and he has not hid his face from him, but has heard, when he cried to him. . . . The afflicted shall eat and be satisfied; those who seek him shall praise the Lord!*
>
> PSALM 22:22-24, 26

"Those who seek shall praise the Lord." What a strange assertion to make from the cross, of all places. But while this is perhaps the most dramatic example, this is hardly the only time Scripture tells us to rejoice in suffering. For example, St. Paul, no stranger to suffering himself, says, "Rejoice in the Lord always; again I will say, Rejoice." (Phil 4:4).

Many people think this verse means we are supposed to put a happy face on our pain, but it does not. It means something much deeper. The Scripture does not say, "Pretend to rejoice." It says, "Rejoice!" The psalm that Jesus prayed on the cross does not say, "Pretend to be satisfied with your lot so that you won't be a downer to everyone else!" It says, "the afflicted . . . *will be* satisfied" (emphasis mine).

But this is possible only if we know the ending of the story—that is to say, if we know the suffering we endure is leading us somewhere. Christ's message to us is that even the most absurd suffering has meaning and a discernible purpose. So when you are despairing in your pain, pray Psalm 22.

Know that your task is not merely to endure the pain cheerfully until it passes—as if anyone could ever do that. Even Jesus didn't do that. Rather, your mission is to embrace the cross, the pain, the suffering, fully, in a way that empowers you, by grace, to discover greater meaning, intimacy, and virtue once the suffering is done. Then, and only then, will you have learned how to join your suffering to the cross of Christ, as Paul tells us in Colossians (see Col 1:24), and be a witness to the world that can inspire us to rejoice in spite of the pain you are experiencing.

The fact is, we know the ending to the story. No matter what this fallen world will throw at you, if you constantly pursue meaningfulness by using your gifts and charisms as fully as possible in your circumstances; intimacy, by sharing with and relating to the people who surround you at this time, as deeply as possible; and virtue, by attempting conscientiously to apply your personal mission statement to whatever circumstances you find yourself in: you will win. Like St. Paul, we will run the race, we will fight the good fight, until the day we have won the crown of life (see 2 Tm 4:7-8).

Whatever pain you are in, whether you are experiencing the loss of a loved one, facing disease, parenting a sick child, confronting financial setbacks, or experiencing the collapse of your dreams, Jesus Christ can give you the grace to be "more than a conqueror" (see Rom 8:37). But you must give up your desire to have things turn out the way you want them to, and instead, tell God that no matter what, you will pursue meaning, intimacy, and virtue.

This is the single most difficult obstacle we experience in overcoming our suffering: giving up the desire to have things turn out the way we want. I think that by and large, this resistance is a healthy thing, because it is our mind's attempt to prevent us from falling into despair. Even so, the resistance we experience to surrendering to God's will is, I believe, based on faulty assumptions about what God's will is. Ultimately, we must make an important distinction between accepting and accommodating ourselves to a miserable situation, and surrendering to God's will.

Find Joy in Surrender

Too often, what people mean when they encourage us to "surrender to God's will" is to keep our heads down and attempt to be content in our misery. If this is really God's will, then it is no wonder that we fight against it so mightily, because it violates the very reason for which we were created.

Jesus did not come to show us how to accommodate ourselves to sin and suffering in the world. He came to give us an example of how to rage against it.

Jesus did not live a quiet, unfulfilled life, keeping his head down, doing work he was not called to do until he died a miserable, quiet little death. His whole life speaks of his fight against sin and suffering. His whole life bears witness to taking healthy risks, saying hard things, and doing noble, fulfilling work. And finally, his Passion, death, and resurrection show us that if we trust in him and follow his example—living defiantly and nobly in the face of sin and suffering—then even if it leads to our earthly doom, God will raise us up and glorify us, just as he did his Son.

To accept our miserable lot and accommodate ourselves to it is exactly the wrong thing to do. Why would Christ need to come to teach us to do what we already do all too naturally? Rather, the call to all Christians is not to accommodate ourselves to suffering, but to embrace it and use it as a tool for our fulfillment.

We must, as Jesus did, fight against the misery the world seeks to put on us. But we must do it in a way that leads to greater meaningfulness, intimacy, and virtue. Sometimes this will be hard. Most of the time, it will involve taking steps we will not want to take and doing what we do not wish to do.

Nevertheless, if we accept this challenge (and really, compared to what the world has to offer, what choice do we have?), then we *truly* surrender to God's will by *surrendering to what must be done to live meaningfully, intimately, and virtuously in spite of the pain that doing so may cause.* If we do this, things may not turn out the way we want them to, but they will turn out even better than they would have had we gotten our way.

Surrendering to God's will means doing what must be done to live meaningfully, intimately, and virtuously so that God, good Father that he is, can give us not just the good things we want, but rather, the best things to be had. Mind you, I don't mean this in merely some mysterious, spiritual sense of what is "best for us." I mean that even while God's will is best for us spiritually, we will also *experience* it as the best of all possibilities for us, if we actually do the work involved in surrendering to that will and fulfilling it. We will find joy in this, because even though so much of us resists it, it is what we were created to do. Happiness results when we function according to the purpose for which we were created.

"God Knows What He Is Doing"

Janice and Paul are the parents of Michael. Michael has Down's syndrome. When Michael was first born, Janice and Paul were angry, depressed, and hopeless about their circumstance.

"It was so surreal," says Janice. "On the one hand, I was thrilled to be a mom. He was such a beautiful baby. But I was angry and sad, too. I remember crying and screaming at God, 'Why? Lord! Why?' But I never got any answers."

Michael's birth was especially hard on Paul. "I went into a fit of depression," he recalls. "Even now, I am completely ashamed of how I acted. I made up reasons to stay at work. I looked for any excuse to be out of the house. I didn't want to have anything to do with either of them.

"I'm not sure why. I guess just looking at Janice and Michael reminded me of all the dreams that I had that would never come true. I couldn't stand looking at them."

Janice says, "It isn't like we ever fought or anything. He just wasn't there, and when he was there, he wasn't there. He wouldn't look at me when I talked to him.

"When I tried to hug him, he wouldn't hug me back. He just kind of stood there with his arms around me. He was completely withdrawn into himself. I didn't have a husband anymore."

Janice was exhausted. With a special needs baby on her hands and an absent husband, she wasn't sure how she was going to make it.

Things got so bad that one night, Paul came home late to find Janice packing. Through her tears, she told him that she couldn't take it anymore. She was leaving.

Paul explains, "It was like, in that moment, I got hit upside the head with a two-by-four. I didn't realize that I had been that big a jerk. I was just trying to get through it the only way I knew how."

Paul begged her to stay. That night, almost nine months after the baby was born, they prayed together for the first time.

"I don't know how it came up," Paul says, "but we prayed right there on the bedroom floor with all her suitcases all around us. I don't even remember what we said. I just know we both cried a lot. We talked really late that night."

Because of that talk, Janice and Paul decided to do several things. First, they decided to pray together every day. Next, they scheduled time every day to check in with how each was feeling and talk about what they needed to do to take care of each other. Finally, they decided to talk to their pastor about getting a referral to a counselor who could help them through the challenges to their marriage.

Janice and Paul faithfully followed their plan, and it made profound changes in their lives. Michael is seven years old now. "I look at our lives now," says Janice, "and I see what an incredible gift Michael is to us. I'm ashamed to say I didn't always feel that way. He is profoundly disabled, and he requires a lot of care and a lot of attention and a lot of time. But he is exactly what we needed in our lives."

"The fact is," says Paul, "our marriage was in trouble long before Michael came along. We were both into living separate lives, doing our own thing. More so me.

"When I look back on it now, I see that I had no idea what it really meant to love somebody. I mean, I loved Janice, but I didn't want to really work at it. You know? I just wanted to 'be together' and let the love flow. Good grief!

"Michael taught me what it really means to love somebody. Michael taught me the importance of just being there, paying attention, working together. I didn't learn that from a book, or my friends, or my work. Michael taught me that, and I love him for it.

"There is nobody who could look at that little boy and tell me that his life has no purpose. He pried open my heart, and he has made Janice and me work harder together than we ever did before."

"We're so close," adds Janice, taking Paul's hand. "I don't know how two people could go through all this together and not become so close. There are days when it's really hard. There are days when I am so sick of changing a seven-year-old's diapers I could cry.

"But I love Michael. And when I look at who I am now, and who I was before we had him—or when I look at our marriage now and how we were before we had him—then I know for us, he is the perfect child. I know that God knows what he is doing."

Paul pauses for a moment before adding: "I've said things like that to people before, and they look at me strangely. Sometimes they've asked me, 'Do you mean that if you could have had it differently, you would choose to have Michael?'

"They don't mean it in any offensive way. I know what they mean, and that's a tough question to answer. If I could have my way, I would want Michael to be well. I would want him to be like all the other kids, 'cause I'm his dad and I want him to have the fullest life possible.

"But if I had to choose between having Michael just as he is, or not having him at all, I would do it all over. Michael is a gift to me. Everything I have, everything I am becoming, is a reality because I had to learn how to be the man Michael and Janice needed me to be."

Janice and Paul are a perfect example of what I was describing earlier. They are an outstanding example of the difference between "accepting their circumstances," which would have resulted in a fatalistic vision of their family, and "surrendering to God's will," which led them to the place they are now. When we confront our suffering, pain, and loss with the will to pursue meaningfulness, intimacy, and virtue in spite of—or because of—our circumstances, God may not give us exactly what we want. But he will give us more than we could have imagined.

EPILOGUE

Finding Strength in Community

Throughout this book, it has been my hope to show you that no matter how far you think your life has strayed from the path God intended you to be on, with his grace, you can find your way back. God created you for a purpose, and with the Lord, you *will* fulfill that purpose, and not even the gates of hell will prevail against you. Living intentionally by pursuing meaningfulness, intimacy, and virtue; practicing the five steps of F.A.I.T.H.; and confronting suffering courageously will allow you to cooperate with God's plan for your life. He will move heaven and earth to help you fulfill the purpose for which you were created.

Before we completely wrap up, though, I would like to take this opportunity to remind you that there is one other thing that we are blessed to have: namely, the help and support of our brothers and sisters in Christ. Even with the tools you have received from this book, it would be a daunting feat to attempt to do most of this work on your own. Genesis tells us that it is not good for us to be alone (see Gn 2:18), and as we discussed in an earlier chapter, every human being depends upon the strength and support of good relationships.

As we conclude, I encourage you to take full advantage of the support your brothers and sisters in Christ can offer. The following pages will briefly examine the sources of some of that support. We will examine how to seek help from the saints, your peers, and professionals.

The Saints

If you can ask for prayer from your friend, your mother, or your cousin, who are no closer to God than you are, why not ask the saints to pray for you as well? They are simply our older brothers and sisters in Christ, devoted to "spend eternity," as St. Therese of Lisieux put it, "doing good on earth."

The saints have been there and done that. You think your life is a mess? Spend some time meditating on St. Augustine, who spent most of his young adulthood living with a woman outside of marriage, fathering a child out of wedlock, and rising in the ranks of a pagan cult. And he is just one of the most notorious examples.

We need to stop thinking of saints as people of pious legend whose feet didn't stink, who never went to the bathroom, or who never had a humorous thought. The Church has a few levitating, bilocating, rose-scented mystics on her list of saints. But they are most definitely in the minority, and even they were thinking, feeling human beings, many of whom had wonderful wits, and all of whom had deep emotional lives.

The saints were very much three-dimensional people who were real in every way. Most saints are people like you and me who struggled mightily against insurmountable odds to work for the good of their neighbor and the glory of God. Who better to pray for you or offer brotherly and sisterly advice on your road to sanctification, fulfillment, and yes, dare I say, holiness?

Your Peers

When we are struggling, we are often afraid to tell the people that could help us most: our friends. *But God did not create us to be alone.*

Pride causes us to close ourselves off from the kindness of the very people God has placed in our life to help. Don't give in to the false thoughts that lead us away from the help God has provided. Talk it over with your friends. They may have important insights for you. And at the least, they can be praying with you and for you.

A Spiritual Director

A good spiritual director can be hard to find. St. Francis de Sales once said they were "one in ten thousand." Yet he or she can be an essential source of spiritual support and accountability, helping you clarify God's will in your life.

Spiritual direction can take many forms. But if your director is a priest, it will most definitely include regular sacramental Confession. Despite the common reluctance people have to make use of this sacrament, it is actually a powerful tool of healing and growth.

Spiritual direction, with or without a priest, may involve heart-to-heart discussions, training in different types of prayer, spiritual reading, and much more. It is a wonderful opportunity to learn how to apply your faith to the tough questions you face every day. It has a way of taking your faith and transforming it from something you do on Sundays, or reserve for special moments in the day, into something that can infuse every minute of your day with meaning and spiritual purpose.

Counseling

Psychotherapy, especially when entered into with a faithful, Catholic Christian counselor, can be a very important resource. If you are struggling to discern God's path for your life, or to overcome the internal or external obstacles that you must face along the road, a competent, faith-filled therapist can be an essential partner in your journey. Though it can be difficult to find a counselor who is both professionally competent and a knowledgeable Christian, I would not trust my emotional, spiritual, and relational health to anyone but a professional who was capable on both fronts.

When seeking such help, in addition to finding someone you like personally, you should find a therapist who will do more than simply have interesting conversations with you. He or she should be focused on giving you new tools to confront the obstacles that stand in your way. An effective therapist should help you define clear, practical goals within the first few sessions.

In fact, most studies demonstrate that the greatest benefit from therapy is achieved within the first twelve weeks of treatment, with steady progress continuing through the next twelve weeks as well. After this period, most of the work tends to be more supportive in nature, with little new and dramatic progress occurring.

Your therapist should be committed to helping you get out of treatment as soon as is reasonably possible. While you should not feel rushed by your counselor, neither should you be made to feel that true progress necessarily takes years. Having said all that, it is possible for more complicated situations to require longer-than-average periods of counseling.

It's Up to You Now

Throughout this book, it has been my hope to provide you with the tools you need to discover joy even in the face of the challenges and disappointments you encounter every day. In these few chapters, you have discovered the meaning of living an abundant life and what it takes to pursue it. You have learned the steps to sound discernment, and you have explored the methods you need to remove the internal and external obstacles that stand in your way.

Finally, you have learned how to remain strong and faithful even in the face of terrible trials. You have seen what it takes to fight back in a godly and effective way when Satan comes after you with all he has to give.

Now it is up to you and the people you choose to help and support you as you continue your mission: to face the disappointments of your life and seek the meaningfulness, intimacy, and virtue that will lead you to the abundant life and the joy that flows from living abundantly.

The psalmist sang to God, you have "turned . . . my mourning into dancing" (Ps 30:11). It is my deepest wish that if you began this book in mourning, you may end it with a renewed spring in your step; that despite your circumstances, you can discover the "peace of God, which passes all understanding" (Phil 4:7)—a peace that St. Paul tells us belongs to all who walk in God's ways, being led by grace into the fullness of God's plan for their lives.

I want to thank you sincerely for allowing me to accompany you this far on your walk to God. I hope that you have found the company to be pleasant, the information useful, and the tone inspiring.

As this book draws to a close, I offer my prayer that you will discover the gifts God has given you; that you will learn to use those gifts fully for the good of others and the glory of God; and that intimacy, virtue, and joy will fill your cup to overflowing.

The Lord bless you and keep you:
The Lord make his face to shine upon you and be gracious to you:
The Lord lift up his countenance upon you,
And give you peace.

NUMBERS 6:24-26

. . . All the days of your life. *Amen.*

About the Author

With eight bestsellers to his name, Dr. Gregory Popcak is one of the country's leading authors in Christian counseling. Cohosting with his wife, Lisa Popcak, Greg brings his unique blend of Christian theology and counseling psychology nationwide with his daily radio call-in program "More to Life," focused on the Theology of the Body. His Pastoral Solutions Institute provides additional telephone counseling and other resources to Catholics worldwide and is the largest organization of its kind in the world.

Timothy M. Gallagher, O.M.V.
Discerning the Will of God
A GUIDE TO CHRISTIAN DECISION MAKING

"How many books have you read on the subject of discerning God's will? Whether it is one or a hundred, you should read this book."

—Matthew Kelly, *New York Times* bestselling author of *The Rhythm of Life* and *The Dream Manager*

"Is it time to change jobs?" "Should I marry?" "Am I called to religious life?" Sooner or later, every thoughtful Christian asks such questions. For everyone ready to make the shift from "What do I want for my life?" to "What does *God* want for my life?" Fr. Gallagher (frtimothygallagher.org), a popular retreat leader and Ignatian scholar, offers this new book to help you make spiritual sense of your major life decisions. Drawing from the timeless methods of Ignatius Loyola and richly illustrated with examples and stories, this book offers practical wisdom for conforming your will to God's will. Fr. Gallagher takes you through each step of the process, including opening your heart to whatever God wants; making use of silence, the Eucharist, Scripture, and spiritual direction; and finding clarity (and what to do when you lack clarity).

While this book focuses on the major decisions such as marriage and career and vocation choices, the insights gained here can be adapted to other significant life decisions as well.

978-0-8245-2489-0, paperback

Also by Gregory K. Popcak
GOD HELP ME!
THESE PEOPLE ARE DRIVING ME NUTS!
Making Peace with Difficult People

Your spouse is driving you crazy, your kids are misbehaving, and the boss is just plain insane. Some days it seems they are everywhere—people intent on making your life miserable. Try as you might, you can't escape them. If you are a Christian, you understand that no matter how much anger and frustration you feel, you must respond to people with the virtues of faith, hope, and love. But how can you do this when people don't respond to you this way? How can you begin to answer the call to love others—*all* others—as God loves us?

God Help Me! is a practical, humorous, and informative book that integrates cutting-edge psychology, case studies, and healing principles. Using the techniques offered by Dr. Greg Popcak, who draws from years of personal and professional experience, you'll discover how to:

— Bring about positive change in your relationships
— Deal with self-destructive people who refuse to change
— Set limits without hurting others
— Love yourself as Christ loves you

"We all talk about the people in our lives who make us want to tear our hair out, but nobody has any clue what to do with them. Greg Popcak is a wonderful antidote to this problem, sharing a wealth of insights and solid wisdom."
— Mark P. Shea, *Making Sense out of Scripture*

978-0-8245-2597-2

Also by Gregory K. Popcak
HOLY SEX!
A Catholic Guide To Toe-Curling, Mind-Blowing, Infallible Loving

"No couple should be without this book. It will transform your marriage."
>—Dan Connors, Editor-in-Chief, *Catholic Digest*

"All who read *Holy Sex!* will find something new and helpful, will laugh a lot, and may even be shocked at what Dr. Popcak reveals to be compatible with Catholic teaching."
>—Janet E. Smith, Sacred Heart Major Seminary

Holy Sex! unveils Christianity's best-kept secret, and does so in an informative, solidly grounded, and delightful way. Want to know your *Holy Sex Quotient*? Ever wonder why Catholics have better sex more often? From a presentation of what the Church really teaches about sex, to *The Infallible Lover's Guide to Pleasure*, Natural Family Planning, and a Q&A on Overcoming Common Problems, this book truly empowers couples to make their marriage last a lifetime.

978-0-8245-2471-5, paperback

Check your local bookstore for availability.
To order directly from the publisher,
please call 1-800-888-4741 for Customer Service
or visit our website at *www.CrossroadPublishing.com.*